Montara Hills
by W. A. Brewer, Jr.

When I am done with city streets
And canyons walled with brick-built towers,
I'll find Montara's still retreats
Among the redwoods* and flowers;
When I am satiated with the new,
I'll go and seek the old, old thrills
That wait all those who wander through
The sleepy, blue Montara Hills!

The redwood armies mount the slope
Knee-deep in tangled underbrush;
Above the dark lakes where fishes grope
To where the span-wide rivers rush;
The drunken bees go blundering by
Blue cups that fragrant honey fills;
You long for these? Then why not try
The sleepy, blue Montara Hills?

Unwaked by gasoline or steam
Untroubled by siren's shrieks,
They still prolong the ancient dream
They dreamed when Spaniards tread their peaks;
To those forespent with cash and change,
But one retreat their hope fulfills,
The old, unwakening redwood range—
The sleepy, blue Montara Hills!
   —April 4, 1925. *San Francisco Bulletin*

---

* Redwoods grow on the eastern slopes only.

[Courtesy Pacific Aerial Surveys]

Pedro Point, San Pedro Mountain and Montara Mountain form a backdrop to San Pedro Rock, which, like an exclamation point, marks where the Santa Cruz Mountains meet the Pacific Ocean. On these slopes, San Pedro Valley County Park, McNee Ranch State Park and Pedro Point headlands (undeveloped) preserve open space in the midst of the San Francisco Peninsula. The Linda Mar district of Pacifica is to the left. The community of Shelter Cove lines the horseshoe bay in the foreground.

Montara Mountain

Stop 4: South of Gray Whale Cove

To get to Stop 4, continue south on Highway One. After 1.6 miles, note Gray Whale Cove State Beach (unmarked) on the right and Gray Whale Cove parking lot on the left. A left turn to the parking lot is difficult. Continue on 0.3 mile to park in one of two adjacent pull-offs on the ocean side of the highway. The second pull-off has an emergency call box.

You cannot help noticing the old World War II U. S. Army bunker standing on a column of rock on top of Gray Whale Cove promontory. The bunker, part of the Harbor Defenses of San Francisco, served as a base-end station. From it, soldiers relayed target sightings to gun batteries north and south of the Golden Gate. In the 1970s, a Texas oil man, intending to build a house, began leveling the property, then gave up the job and returned to Texas. The bunker on the rock is a monument to his folly. The promontory is off-limits for hiking.

The World War II bunker atop a column of rock at Gray Whale Cove. Devil's Slide promontory is in the distance.

At the pull-off, look directly behind you to note the road cut, Highway One and the speeding cars. Look on page 138 to see the same road cut and an Ocean Shore Railroad train. Above the highway is Gray Whale Cove Trail in McNee Ranch State Park, which is on the old Half Moon Bay–Colma Road. To the north, far in the distance, you can see the continuation of the old road as it hairpins its way up the ridge of Devil's Slide promontory.

On bright spring days, inevitably someone at this pull-off will spot what they think is an oil slick offshore. The oil slick is actually the spring bloom of red algae, which thrives on long days of sunshine and the seasonal upwelling of nutrient-rich ocean currents. Red tides are harmless to people.

Drive along Devil's Slide

As you drive past Devil's Slide promontory (no hiking and no parking allowed) note the steep stairs leading to trees and an observation tower on the top. The U. S. Army acquired this 9.61-acre promontory from Hibernia Bank in 1939, along with the 13.7-acre promontory at Gray Whale Cove, for Harbor Defenses of San Francisco base-end stations. Base-end stations were fortified triangulation points. During World War II, soldiers took readings on the position of targets they sighted offshore and telephoned the information to gun batteries north and south of the Golden Gate. Old soldiers remember that their readings from these stations were used only to pinpoint practice targets, never Japanese ships. During the war, long caravans of military vehicles frequently plied Highway One between the Presidio of San Francisco and the Presidio of Monterey.

Montara Mountain has three World War II bunker sites: Gray Whale Cove promontory, Devil's Slide promontory and the south ridge of Green Valley (see pages 46–47). All were abandoned by the Army in the late 1940s.

> **Monaco West**
> In 1963, Montara resident Alfred J. Wiebe bought the 9.61-acre Devil's Slide promontory as war surplus. He planned to build apartments, a spa, a restaurant and a castle with a radio station—all on top of the promontory. In 1968, he took the press and other visitors up the 200 reinforced concrete and steel steps to the top of the rock to show off abandoned gun emplacements, views and his plans. Wiebe told everyone,
>
>> "I was alerted to this majestic and rugged area by Princess Charlotte Magnette of France and Belgium—now living in El Granada—who claimed the area outdid the Côte d'Azur in Monaco. The Devil's Slide development will be named 'Monaco West.'" [3]
>
> The Princess planned to take photos of a castle in France which she thought would look good atop the promontory. She also planned to buy the surrounding 1,200 acres and build a ten million dollar yacht harbor.

---

[3] February 28, 1968. *Burlingame Advance–Star*

Earthquakes also can be hard on Devil's Slide. There are at least five inactive faults along the Slide. In addition, San Andreas Fault is four miles to the north and Seal Cove fault at Moss Beach is three miles to the south. After the San Francisco earthquake of 1906, geologists reported,

> "Near San Pedro Point there was a large movement of the earth on the face of the high cliff. One earth-avalanche to the north of the Devil's Slide [the promontory] started at 800 feet above the shore and swept the face of the cliff, carrying away several hundred feet of [Ocean Shore Railroad] roadbed. The slide occurred near the contact of sandstones reposing on granite, and both kinds of rock were involved."[1]

On October 17, 1989, at 5:04 PM, my husband was driving on Devil's Slide, coming home to El Granada. He never felt the Loma Prieta earthquake. It seems that Devil's Slide can either be badly shaken by an earthquake on the San Andreas Fault—or not shaken at all.

Devil's Slide Lore

Legend has it that Devil's Slide is a good place to dump a body. The county sheriff once said,

> "No man will ever know how many were killed there—tossed to the sharks with a bullet in the head."[2]

Cars and trucks have gone over the edge of the Slide—generally because of speed, alcohol and/or drugs. Once, a car was purposefully pushed over the edge during the filming of the 1960 movie, *Portrait in Black*. Lana Turner and Anthony Quinn drove to the Slide to push over a car with Lloyd Nolan's body in it.

No one has ever been killed because of a landslide at Devil's Slide. No one was killed in building the highway at Devil's Slide. In 1911, the Ocean Shore Railroad lost a road foreman in a landslide at Pedro Point tunnel.

Local lore has it that Highway One was the scene of countless gangland killings and body dumps during the Prohibition years (1920–1933). But Highway One didn't open until 1937. Any body dumping would have been from the abandoned Ocean Shore roadbed.

---

[1] Lawson. p. 387.
[2] September 14, 1967. *Half Moon Bay Review*

Drive along Devil's Slide

have driven past the Tobin depot, around Shelter Cove, through the tunnel and along the rock ledge on the south side of Pedro Point. Highway One opened in 1937.

Jagged Pedro Point has seen its share of shipwrecks. In 1876, the *Rydall Hall*, a ship made of iron and loaded with coal, crashed on the rocks. In 1881, the *Alice Birch*, bound for Portland with a load of railroad iron, went ashore. In 1910, the *James Rolph*, a four-masted schooner bound for Australia, went aground on the rocks, a stone's throw from the Ocean Shore Railroad track. For weeks, passengers on the train watched the ship disintegrate.

[Courtesy California Department of Transportation]
Highway One crossing the San Pedro Mountain ocean bluffs. The unstable 1,000-foot-long section—called Devil's Slide—is in the middle of the photo. A slight trace of the Ocean Shore Railroad roadbed is visible below the highway.

Winter rains can be hard on the 1,000-foot-long section of Devil's Slide. A heavy soaking can cause slope failure in the weak shale and sandstone above the highway. The resulting landslides have closed Highway One for days. The rocks below the highway are much more resistant to erosion, including wave erosion. This section of Highway One is the center of a great deal of controversy: Should a 4.5-mile-long new highway be built one mile inland to bypass Devil's Slide, or should the present highway and bluffs be moved just a few hundred feet inland to stabler rock? (See pages 165–168.) Landslides are less frequent south of the Saddle Cut: The rock is erosion-resistant, coarse-grained granite.

would not be crashing on the rocks below you. Instead, you would have to walk to the Farallon Islands, now twenty-five miles offshore, to hear the waves. At that time, much of the oceans' waters were frozen up in glaciers; sea levels were quite low and coastal terraces very broad. Five thousand years ago, the shoreline looked much the same as it does today: The Ice Age was over, the glaciers melted and the Farallons became the islands that we know.

Ocean Shore Railroad trains once puffed along the rocky ledge on Pedro Point. The tunnel was near the tip of the point. San Pedro Rock attracts thousands of sea birds who leave behind nutrient-rich white guano. The guano accumulates during the dry months, covering up the stripes in the rock, and washes away in the winter rains. In the near future, the Pedro Point headlands will be parkland open to the public.

Look along Pedro Point to trace the slim eroded ledge that was once the roadbed of the Ocean Shore Railroad. The roadbed slices across the face of San Pedro Mountain at an angle just below your feet, slowing gaining elevation to join Highway One at the Saddle Cut ahead. South from the Saddle Cut to Martini Creek, Highway One uses the old roadbed and road cuts of the Ocean Shore railroad—except at Green Valley where the railroad looped inland a bit and the highway crosses the valley on a dike.

In the 1930s, when the State started acquiring the railroad right of way for Highway One, the Ocean Shore Railroad refused to relinquish Pedro Point. Consequently, highway engineers surveyed a new route, the road you have just driven. If the Ocean Shore had relinquished Pedro Point, to take this tour you would

Drive along Devil's Slide

Stop 3: Devil's Slide

To get to Stop 3, return to Highway One via Kent Road or San Pedro Avenue. Turn right on Highway One and proceed uphill 1.2 miles. Pull off at the curve above the ocean near the emergency call box.

On the way from Stop 2 to Stop 3, Highway One circles around the recently acquired park, Pedro Point headlands. Historic Shamrock Ranch, with horse boarding stables and dog kennels, is in the narrow valley below the highway. On the far slope of the valley, note the old Half Moon Bay–Colma Road, which was used to cross the mountain from 1879 until 1915.

Highway One goes through the Coastal Scrub plant community. The gray-green shrubs are Coast Sagebrush, the bright green shrubs Coyote Bush. In the spring and summer look for these flowers growing from the rocky road cuts: bright pink Farewell-to-Spring, bright yellow Gum Plant, and mustard-yellow Sticky Monkey Flower.

Layers of sandstone and shale exposed by the Highway One road cut.

At the pull-off, the ocean and mountain views take your breath away. You are now on the south side of Pedro Point. To your left, the San Pedro Mountain bluffs, at 900 feet above sea level, drop abruptly to the ocean. The pull-off is at 465 feet. Behind you, the Highway One road cut exposes thin, contorted layers of shale and sandstone that 60 million years ago lay flat on the ocean floor. Twenty thousand years ago, if you stood on this spot, the ocean

Montara Mountain

In the 1880s, travellers on the Half Moon Bay–Colma Road along the bluff top named the chute-like ridge, which ended in a domed promontory, "Devil's Slide." The Ocean Shore Railroad blasted the Saddle Cut, now used by Highway One, through the ridge.

Names

Devil's Slide is a slippery name. Some folks apply it to the whole face of San Pedro Mountain—from the pull-off for Stop 3 to the Highway One Saddle Cut adjacent to the massive promontory to the south. Others apply it only to the geologically unstable 1,000-foot-long section of ocean bluffs marked along the highway by caution signs and white concrete barriers.

However, the name Devil's Slide came into use long before anyone thought of building a railroad or a highway along these bluffs.

Originally Devil's Slide meant only the promontory and its inland ridge. In the 1880s, travellers in horse-drawn wagons on the Half Moon Bay–Colma Road, which ran along the top of the ocean bluffs, paused to note the chute-like ridge ending in the massive rock dome. They thought it looked fit for a Devil's Slide and named it so.

The Ocean Shore Railroad blasted through the ridge for its roadbed and called the notch the Saddle Cut. The railroad never used the name Devil's Slide for the landslide-prone section of San Pedro Mountain. It is only in recent times, with the building of Highway One across the unstable bluffs, that the name Devil's Slide has come to mean the ocean face of the mountain.

Some maps use "Devils Slide" but most folks use "Devil's Slide."

Drive along Devil's Slide

Stop 2: Shelter Cove on Pedro Point

To get to Stop 2, go back one block from the Tobin depot and turn uphill on Kent Road off Danmann Avenue. Wind 0.5 mile through San Pedro Terrace tract. Parking above Shelter Cove is limited to three cars on Blackburn Terrace off the end of Kent Road.

Shelter Cove, population 30, is the most isolated community in the Bay Area. The road into the cove—the old Ocean Shore Railroad roadbed—washed out in the fierce winter storms of 1982. Residents park their cars near the Tobin depot and walk in and out, carrying groceries and garbage. An old truck, lowered with a winch down this slope in 1989, transports heavy items from the washout to the cottages. All eighteen cottages, built in the 1930s, are rentals—and there is a long waiting list for vacancies. During the Prohibition years (1920-1933), the large two-story building was a restaurant and speak-easy. At night, rumrunners took over the cove, known then as Smugglers Cove, to off-load thousands of bottles of illegal whiskey from Canadian ships. The next day the whiskey was for sale in San Francisco speak-easies. After Prohibition, the building became a store and museum, called The Clipper Ship, which displayed paintings of old ships and curiosities of the sea.

Directly below you, on the ledge above the cottages, is the old Ocean Shore roadbed. You can trace the roadbed along Pedro Point to the tunnel entrance, where trains gave a last toot before disappearing into 354 feet of darkness. Prohibition agents blasted the tunnel shut in the late 1920s—too many smugglers stored their goods there.

Pedro Point headlands, between the ocean and Highway One, recently became public land. Once used by a motorcycle club, the badly scarred and eroded slopes will need much restoration before people can hike the trails. When opened, the 246-acre park will offer unbeatable views from the San Mateo County coast to Point Reyes.

Pedro Point and striped San Pedro Rock just offshore compose the coastal trademark of Pacifica. In 1993, residents held an art festival featuring paintings and photographs of their beloved Pedro Point.

Montara Mountain

Shelter Cove. Ocean Shore Railroad trains used to puff along the ledge just behind the cottages on the beach.

Power lines to the beach community of Shelter Cove frame the view of Pedro Point where the Ocean Shore Railroad tunnel once pierced the mountain. San Pedro Rock is just offshore.

Stop 1: Tobin Depot on Pedro Point

From Highway One at Linda Mar Boulevard, go 0.2 mile south and turn right on San Pedro Avenue (marked). Go 0.2 mile to Danmann Avenue. Turn right and go two blocks to the end of the street. Park in front of the Pedro Point Firehouse, or turn left and park on the old Ocean Shore Railroad roadbed next to the Tobin depot, which is now a private house.

Thanks to the Ocean Shore Railroad, which ran along the San Mateo County coast from 1907 until 1920, Pedro Point today has streets and houses. Speculators laid out the suburban tract of San Pedro Terrace shortly before the first train from San Francisco arrived at Tobin station on October 2, 1907. On board were 125 prospective lot buyers who enjoyed the sun and sand at what was to be "A San Francisco Sea Side Resort." Tobin station took its name from the Tobin family, owners of Pedro Point and founders of Hibernia Bank.

Tobin depot sits on the ocean side of the Ocean Shore roadbed. You can walk along a bit of the roadbed dike as it curves around the bay. Legend has it that parallel dark bands on the road surface mark the position of the old railroad ties. Look across the bay to Rockaway Point. There, a faint rock ledge marks the route of the Ocean Shore as it rounded the point. At one time, farmers in San Pedro Valley, now the Linda Mar district of Pacifica, grew some of the world's finest artichokes, which were shipped to San Francisco on the Ocean Shore Railroad from Tobin station. San Pedro Creek, one of the few remaining Steelhead Trout spawning creeks in San Mateo County, enters the ocean near the eroded end of the dike.

At Tobin, Ocean Shore trains began their journey around Pedro Point. The old roadbed along the bluff face collapsed during the winter storms of 1982. Walk to the chain-link fence. The signs say "Tenant Parking Only" and "No Trespassing." Yes, people do live beyond the fence in the community of Shelter Cove, located on a lovely, tiny, horseshoe-shaped bay. A drive to Stop 2 will give you a view of Shelter Cove. (See frontispiece for aerial view of Shelter Cove and the roadbed of the Ocean Shore Railroad around Pedro Point.)

Montara Mountain

Tobin depot, now a private house, was the last passenger stop on the Ocean Shore Railroad before the trains crossed San Pedro Mountain and Montara Mountain. (See page 134 for a look at the depot during the days of the Ocean Shore Railroad.)

The old Ocean Shore roadbed curves part of the way around the bay of Pacifica State Beach. (See page 134 for a view of the bay during the days of the Ocean Shore Railroad.)

~2~

A Drive along Devil's Slide

The 5.1-mile drive along Devil's Slide on Highway One has five stops. To begin your journey drive to the intersection of Linda Mar Boulevard and Highway One in Pacifica. Since the legal pull-offs along Devil's Slide are on the ocean side of the highway, a drive from north to south is recommended.

    Devil's Slide is one of the best-known landmarks on the San Mateo County coast. A drive on Highway One along the Slide is exhilarating and inspiring. Where else can you witness such a meeting of ocean, land and sky?
    The 5.1-mile drive takes you from an old Ocean Shore Railroad depot to a Native American Costano shell midden. It takes you from the sheer shale and sandstone ocean face of San Pedro Mountain to the rugged granite ocean face of Montara Mountain.
    On your journey you will pass three state beaches: Pacifica State Beach, Gray Whale Cove State Beach and Montara State Beach; and two parks: San Pedro Point headlands (undeveloped) and McNee Ranch State Park. (San Pedro Valley County Park is inland from Highway One.) After your drive, plan to return to enjoy the beaches and the mountain trails.

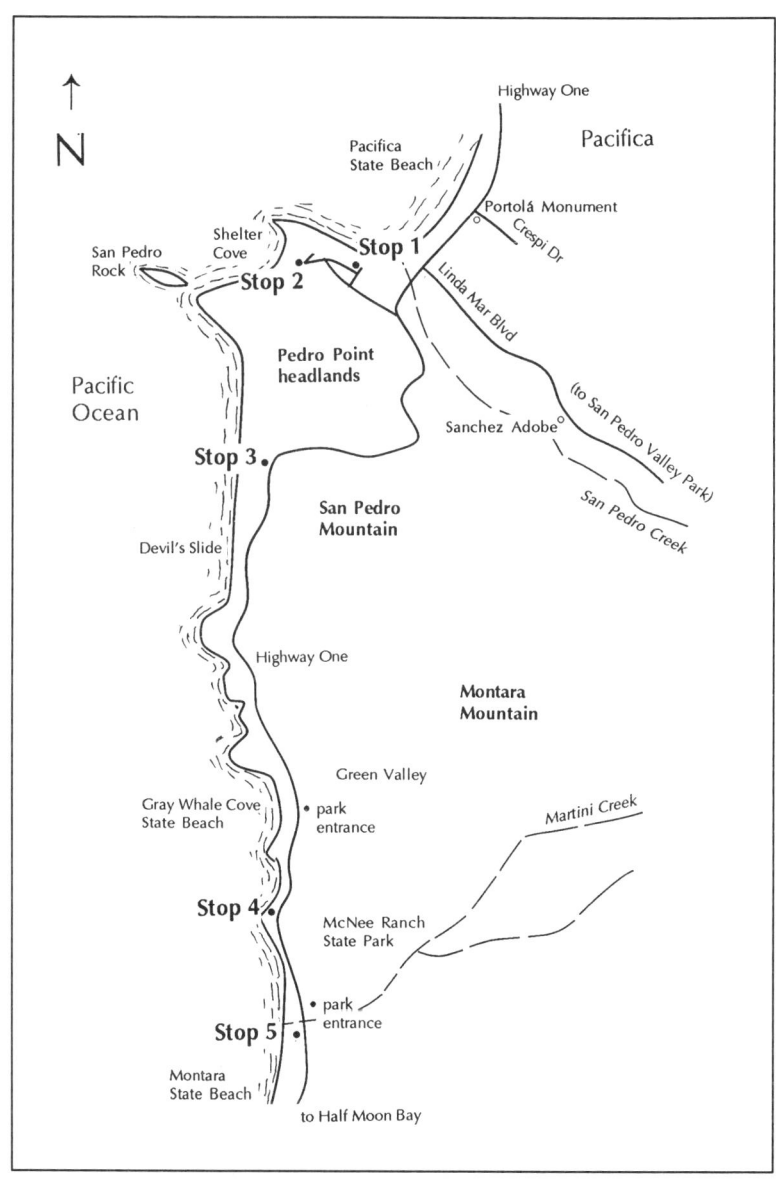

A drive along Devil's Slide.

Montara Mountain

> They don't make mountains like Montara Mountain anymore.

- Montara Mountain has experienced minimal human impact other than roads, pastures and grain fields.
- Montara Mountain is a plant island. The special combination of Coastal Scrub and Coastal Chaparral found on its slopes grows no place else on earth.
- Steelhead trout spawn in San Pedro Creek, which begins high on the northern slopes of Montara Mountain.
- Montara Mountain and Mt. Tamalpais in Marin County provide the only ocean-to-mountain hiking in the Bay Area.
- Montara Mountain is the barrier that has kept the San Mateo County coast rural. In the early years of this century, San Franciscans chose to settle the accessible bayside of the Peninsula.
- Sweeney Ridge, a spur of Montara Mountain and part of the Golden Gate National Recreation Area, has been called the Plymouth Rock of the West Coast. It is from Sweeney Ridge, after crossing Montara Mountain, that the Spanish sighted San Francisco Bay and made plans for the settlement of California.

Names
Montara is a made-up word that originated when somebody misread a map. An 1838 map labeled the valley of the south fork of San Pedro Creek *Cañada Montosa* (wooded valley). The next mapmaker (in the 1850s) misspelled the name and applied it to the mountain, hence Montara Mountain.

Green Valley and the Saddle Pass separate Montara Mountain from San Pedro Mountain.

San Pedro Mountain is named after a Spanish agriculture outpost located in San Pedro Valley in the 1780s. The full name of the outpost was *San Pedro y San Pablo*.

Coastside refers to the mid-coast region of San Mateo County, stretching south from Montara Mountain to Half Moon Bay. People who live here call themselves Coastsiders.

North Coast refers to the town of Pacifica, north of Montara Mountain. People who live here call themselves both Pacificans and Coastsiders.

Montara Mountain

[Courtesy San Mateo County Harbor District]

Montara Mountain, which pours steeply into the Pacific Ocean, separates the northern San Francisco Peninsula coast from the southern. Historically, people have regarded Montara Mountain as a barrier to be crossed. Now, people regard Montara Mountain as an island of plant and animal diversity and a serene open space to be preserved. Montara Mountain is a Bay Area treasure.

–1–

Montara Mountain

Montara Mountain—the name alone evokes measured majesty. A glimpse of its granite ocean bluffs, narrow ridges and three peaks lifts your spirits. A hike on its trails refreshes your soul. Its ocean views take your breath away. Poets have described Montara Mountain as "beetle-browed" and "brooding," and as "a gray-green granite hulk." The mountain is also sunshine and shadows, and unforgettable fragrances. It is where land, ocean and sky meet like no place else on earth. No one knows what Native Americans called Montara Mountain but surely their name was as pleasing as ours to utter.

    Montara Mountain,[*] along with San Pedro Mountain, forms the northern spur of the Santa Cruz Mountains, the long narrow range which separates the bayside of the San Francisco Peninsula from the coastside. We are lucky to have so much of the two mountains in public hands. Three parks preserve most of the slopes: San Pedro Valley County Park, McNee Ranch State Park and Pedro Point headlands (undeveloped). Three state beaches line the coast: Pacifica State Beach, Gray Whale Cove State Beach and Montara State Beach.

    Yet, Montara Mountain is in trouble: It is the center of one of the most acrimonious land-use battles in the Bay Area. For the past three and one-half decades the issue of building a highway—called the Devil's Slide Bypass—over the mountain has pitted neighbor against neighbor, citizens against government agencies, and slow-growthers against developers. At stake is one of the few remaining natural wildlands on the Peninsula—a mountain which has seen minimal human impact, a mountain which supports great biological diversity, and a mountain which offers tranquility to all who visit its slopes.

    Hike Montara Mountain and decide for yourself what its fate should be.

---

[*] The name Montara Mountain is often used to include San Pedro Mountain.

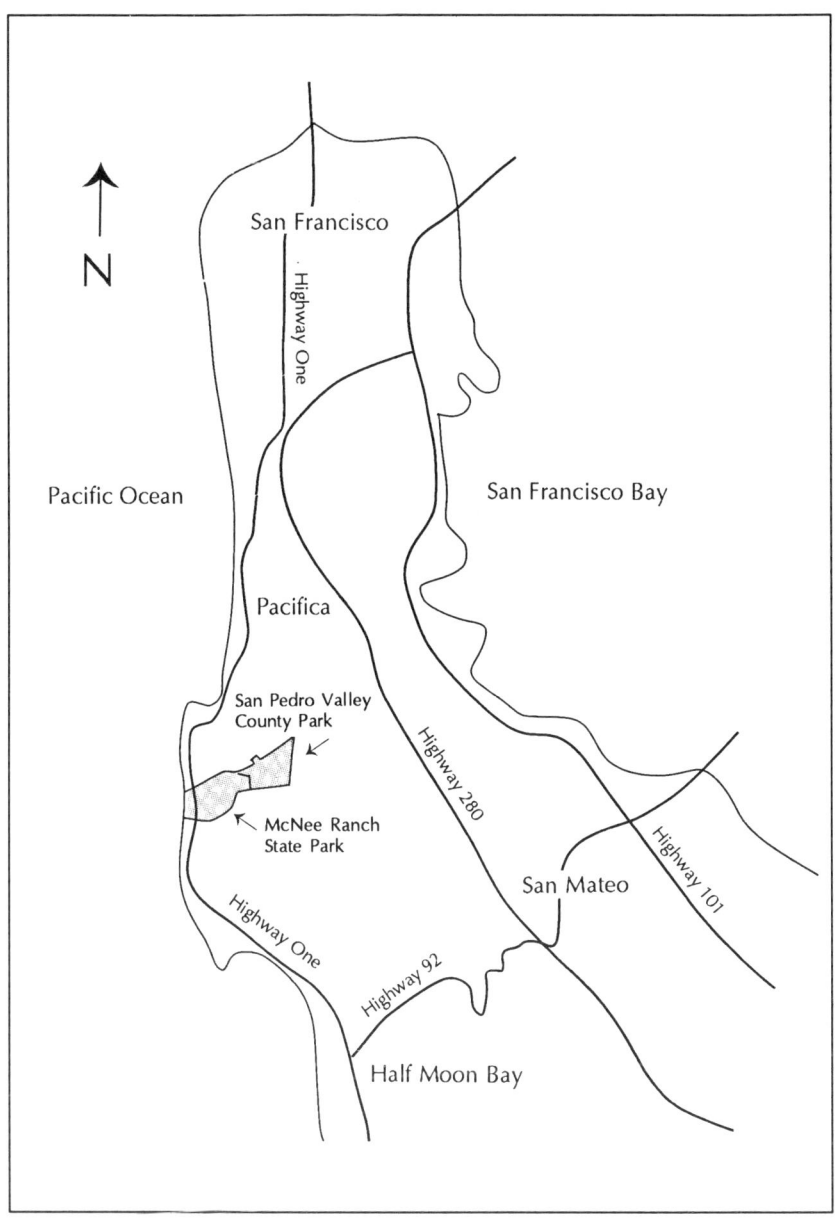

San Pedro Valley County Park and McNee Ranch State Park offer spectacular hiking on Montara Mountain on the San Mateo County coast.

Contents

1	Montara Mountain	7
2	A Drive along Devil's Slide	11
3	San Pedro Valley County Park	25
4	McNee Ranch State Park	39
5	Plants of Montara Mountain	55
	White Flowers	61
	Yellow Flowers	72
	Red Flowers	79
	Brown to Green Flowers	86
	Blue Flowers	87
	Trees	93
	Ferns	99
	Grasses	101
6	Wildlife of Montara Mountain	103
7	Crossings of Montara Mountain	115
	Native American	116
	Spanish	117
	Mexican	119
	Road Trail	121
	Half Moon Bay–Colma Road	123
	Ocean Shore Railroad	131
	Coastside Boulevard	145
	Highway One	155
	Modified Marine Disposal Alternative or Devil's Slide Bypass	165
	Helpful Books	169
	Index	170

Montara Mountain

© Copyright 1994 by Barbara VanderWerf. All rights reserved. No part of this book may be reproduced or utilized in any form or by any means without permission in writing, except for brief quotations embodied in critical articles or reviews.

Printed and bound in the United States of America.

ISBN: 0-9632922-2-6

Library of Congress Catalog Card Number: 94–76133

9 8 7 6 5 4 3 2 1

Many thanks to the following for their generous help:
Ranger Chet Bardo, McNee Ranch State Park
Ranger Dennis Hanley, San Pedro Valley County Park
San Mateo County Historical Association
Shirley Drye, Naturalist
Ted Wurm, Railroad Historian
Vernon Sappers, Railroad Historian
Duncan Nanney, Ocean Shore Railroad Historian
Jim Husing, Pacific Bus Museum
Bob Burrowes, Bus Historian
Ben Pease, Trail Center

Acknowledgements: I am deeply indebted to Roger Raiche for his Montara Mountain plant lists.

As always, for Bill, Joel and Martha.

For a complete trail map of Sweeney Ridge and Montara Mountain, contact
    The Trail Center
    3291 East Bayshore
    Palo Alto, CA 94303
    (415) 968–7065

Every attempt has been made to insure the accuracy of the trail information for San Pedro Valley County Park and McNee Ranch State Park and the road information for Pedro Point roads and Highway One. The author and publisher assumes no responsibility for the condition of the trails in San Pedro Valley County Park and McNee Ranch State Park, for the condition of the roads on Pedro Point, for the condition of Highway One, or for injuries to users of roads and trails described in this book. Please hike and drive safely.

Please mail comments and suggestions to—
    Gum Tree Lane Books
    P.O. Box 1574
    El Granada, CA 94018

Cover photo: Montara Mountain in McNee Ranch State Park.

Montara Mountain

•San Pedro Valley County Park •McNee Ranch State Park
•Devil's Slide •Trails •Plants •Animals •Historical Lore
•San Mateo County Coast

Barbara VanderWerf

Gum Tree Lane Books
El Granada, California

> **Warning**
> **Hiking or Climbing**
> **Prohibited in this Area**
> This property is designated as a dangerous area.
> It shall be unlawful to trespass thereon.
> San Mateo County Ordinance No. 1462

You may also see the San Mateo County Sheriff Department Rescue Unit practicing cliff rescues from this parking lot. Even though there are warning signs, reckless folks try to scamper down the sheer rock face to the beach below. This is not a new problem. In 1949, the warning signs read,

> Warning! Dangerous! Do not go on the beach.
> While fishing on these beaches, 10 people have lost their lives.
> Do you want to be number 11?

Stop 5: Montara State Beach

To get to Stop 5, continue south on Highway One 0.6 mile to the first Montara State Beach parking lot (unmarked). The entrance to McNee Ranch State Park is to your left just before the right-hand turn to Montara State Beach. (See pages 39–51 for McNee Ranch State Park trail information.)

Or, return to Gray Whale Cove State Beach (clothing optional beach), the only beach access between Pacifica State Beach and Montara State Beach.

Highway One descends from Montara Mountain to a broad fertile coastal terrace. Once, the sight of thousands of artichoke plants greeted travellers to the Coastside. Today, the field of Brussels sprouts and peas at the foot of Montara Mountain only hints at the abundance that once was.

At Montara State Beach, Martini Creek, which drains Montara Mountain, flows year-round next to the steps that lead to the shore. The yellow beach sand was once yellow granite rock on the slopes of Montara Mountain. The parking lot is adjacent to a Native American Costano shell midden.

Enjoy the rest of the day at the beach, or cross the highway to the park entrance for McNee Ranch State Park and choose a trail to hike.

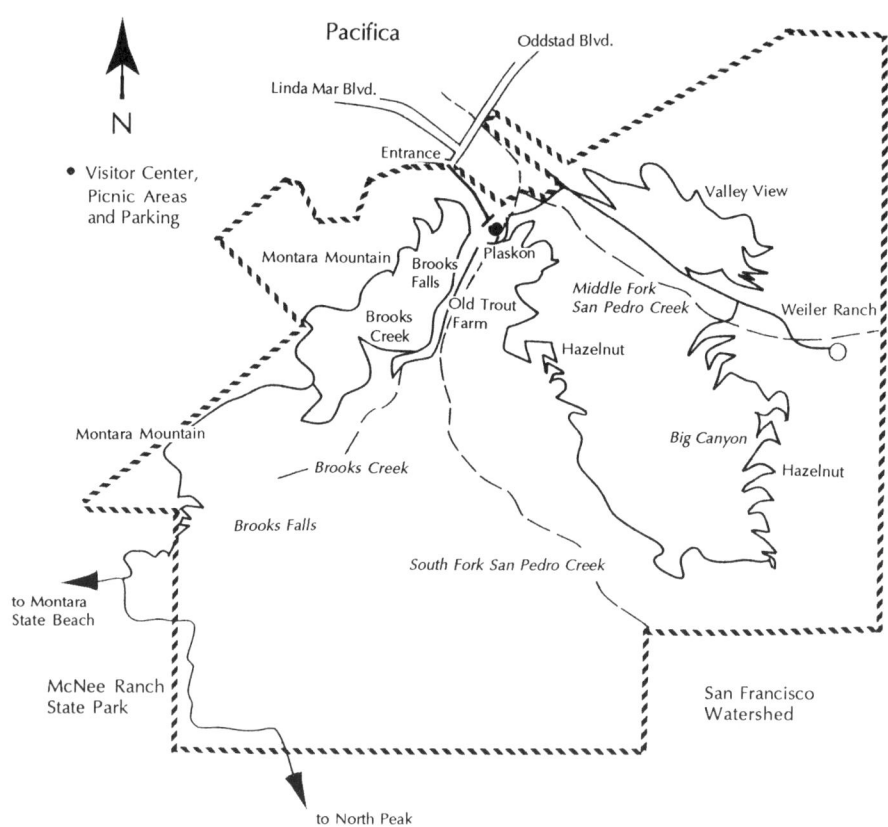

San Pedro Valley County Park Trails

Plaskon Nature Trail: 400 feet one way. Easy.
Old Trout Farm Trail: 0.3 mile one way. Easy.
Brooks Falls Overlook Trail: 0.6 mile one way. Moderate.
Brooks Creek Trail: 0.8 mile one way. Rigorous.
Montara Mountain Trail: 2.1 miles one way. Rigorous.
Weiler Ranch Road: 1.0 mile one way. Easy.
Valley View Trail: 1.4 miles one way. Moderate.
Hazelnut Trail: 3.7 miles one way. Rigorous.

Wear sturdy shoes on the rigorous trails (especially Montara Mountain Trail). Take along water and a jacket. At higher elevations, the fog and wind can come up suddenly.

Park maps and nature guides are available at the Visitor Center.

—3—

San Pedro Valley County Park

San Pedro Valley County Park in Pacifica is a 1,150-acre jewel in the chain of San Mateo County parks. The park offers fine hiking through rich and diverse Coastal Scrub and Coastal Chaparral vegetation and along year-round creeks. When the rest of the San Mateo County coast is foggy, you can hike the park's sunny valley and watch the fog pour over the mountain tops. Or, on brilliant sunny days, you can hike to the mountain tops and enjoy spectacular views of the Pacific Ocean, San Mateo County, San Francisco and Marin County.

In the spring, the wildflowers—especially along Hazelnut Trail—are abundant and magnificently varied. In all seasons and on all trails, walk quietly to observe the wildlife, from Mule Deer to Merriam Chipmunks, and from Scrub Jays to Wrentits.

Be sure to stop at the Visitor Center, which is staffed by welcoming San Pedro Valley Park Volunteers. You'll enjoy the nature exhibits, the library and the exceptional collection of pressed flowers. And don't miss the observation platform overlooking the South Fork of San Pedro Valley Creek, just off the patio.

San Pedro Valley County Park is especially popular with families. The park shares a boundary with McNee Ranch State Park.

The Visitor Center at San Pedro Valley County Park.

San Pedro Valley County Park

Where: 600 Oddstad Boulevard, Pacifica, CA 94044. Take Highway One to Linda Mar Boulevard. Turn inland and continue for two miles until Linda Mar Boulevard ends at Oddstad Boulevard. Turn right and then immediately left at the park entrance.

By bus, take SamTrans 1L or 1C to Linda Mar Boulevard and transfer to 10L. Get off at Linda Mar and Oddstad Boulevard and walk into the park. For schedules, call SamTrans 1-800-660-4BUS.

Telephone: (415) 355-8289.

Admission Charge: Weekends only.

Hours: Daily from 8 AM to sunset.

Visitor Center: Museum, library, bookstore. Open Saturdays and Sundays from 10 AM to 4 PM.

Hiking Trails: Range from easy (400 feet) to rigorous (3.7 miles).

Wheelchair Accessible: Most trails are wheelchair accessible, ranging from short, flat trails (Level 4) to rigorous mountain trails requiring mountain chairs (Level 1). Wheelchairs are available at no charge in the Visitor Center (weekends only).

Bicycle Trail: Weiler Ranch Road is the only bicycle trail in the park. Slight incline. Gravel surface. 1.0 mile one way. Suitable for children. **Bicycles are not allowed on any other trail in the park.**

Horses: All trails except Brooks Creek Trail and Brooks Falls Overlook Trail.

Trout Farm Picnic Area: No reservations required.

Walnut Grove Group Picnic Area: Reservations required. Phone (415) 363-4021.

Dogs or Other Pets: No.

Fishing: No.

San Pedro Valley County Park Volunteers: Meet at 7 PM on the second Wednesday of every month at the Visitor Center. Meet at 8 AM on the second Saturday of every month to work on trails. Phone (415) 355-5454.

San Pedro Valley County Park

Plaskon Nature Trail

> **Length:** 400 feet (one way). Easy trail.
> **Trailhead:** To the right (south) of the Visitor Center.
> **Wheelchair Accessible:** Slight incline. Gravel surface. Designed for the disabled. Level 4.
> **Visually Impaired Accessible:** Redwood handrail along length of trail.
> **Bench:** Yes.
> **Note:** *Nature Trail Guide* pamphlets available at the trailhead and at the Visitor Center.

Trail Notes

Plaskon Nature Trail, a lush creekside trail, is perfect for leisurely bird watching and plant identification.

Two bridges wind you across the South Fork of San Pedro Creek, which flows year-round. From the bridge near the trailhead, look for Western Chain Fern, Lady Fern, Sword Fern and Coast Wood Fern. From the bridge at the trail's end, note the stick which measures yearly high-water marks.

Between December and March, you may see silvery-gray Steelhead Trout as they migrate from the ocean up San Pedro Creek to spawn. Steelhead Trout, actually native Coastal Rainbow Trout that spend their adult lives in the ocean, always return to spawn in the freshwater stream where they hatched. Young Steelhead swim downstream during the summer months to join others in the salty Pacific. San Pedro Creek supports one of the few remaining steelhead populations in San Mateo County.

In February and March, look along the trail for the earliest spring flowers in the park—Fetid Adder's Tongue, Coast Trillium and Giant Trillium. Creek Dogwood is in blossom by April. Note its shiny red branches year-round. A Coast Live Oak arches over the trail just past the first bridge.

Chestnut-backed Chickadees and Anna's Hummingbirds are common throughout the year.

Western Chain Fern

Old Trout Farm Trail

Length: 0.3 mile (one way). Easy trail.
Trailhead: Trout Farm Picnic Area.
Wheelchair Accessible: Six-foot-wide trail, slight incline. Level 4.
Bench: No.
Bicycles: No.
Horses: Yes.
Note: Old Trout Farm Trail connects with Brooks Falls Overlook Trail for a 0.9-mile loop hike. Brooks Falls Overlook Trail is not wheelchair accessible.

Trail Notes

Old Trout Farm Trail takes you along the South Fork of San Pedro Creek. Over the years, several commercial trout farms lined the South Fork, the most recent being John Gay's Trout Farm. The devastating Linda Mar flood of 1958 silted up Gay's trout ponds, killing over 25,000 fish. Shortly after the flood, San Mateo County began acquiring the property for the park. San Pedro Creek last flooded in 1982.

The road beyond the locked gate at the end of Old Trout Farm Trail winds up the South Fork to North Coast County Water District Property and the source of some of Pacifica's drinking water.

The shaded bank of San Pedro Creek offers excellent bird watching. In April and May, enjoy the display of Creek Dogwood in bloom along the trailside.

The lush dell where Old Trout Farm Trail meets Brooks Falls Overlook Trail.

Brooks Falls Overlook Trail

Length: 0.6 mile (one way). Moderate trail.
Elevation Change: 200 feet to 350 feet.
Trailhead: Near restrooms in Trout Farm Picnic Area.
Wheelchair Accessible: No.
Bench: Yes.
Bicycles: No.
Horses: No.
Note: Brooks Falls Overlook Trail connects with Old Trout Farm Trail for a 0.9-mile loop hike.

Trail Notes

Brooks Falls Overlook Trail leads you to Brooks Creek but doesn't give you a good view of Brooks Falls. For a view of the Falls, take Brooks Creek Trail, which forks off to the right after 0.5 mile.

Brooks Falls Overlook Trail passes through a man-made grove, planted with a Coast Redwood here, a Douglas Fir there, and Monterey Pines and Blue Gum Eucalyptus everywhere. Especially noteworthy are the ancient pillar-like Blue Gums which march down Brooks Creek near the end of the trail.

In the early spring, enjoy some of the park's first trailside wildflowers: Milkmaids (February), and Hound's Tongue, Fringe Cups and Coast Trillium (March).

The trail skirts the remains of the old Brooks summerhouse, which burned down in 1956. Note the cobblestone steps leading to nowhere. The Brooks family built and lived in the present-day Ranger's residence located just uphill from the trailhead.

Walk on through a lovely secluded dell until you come out on Old Trout Farm Trail, which leads back to the picnic area.

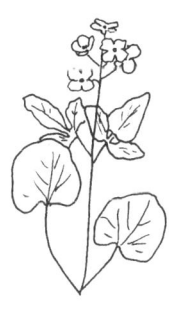

Milkmaids

Montara Mountain

Brooks Creek Trail

> **Length:** 0.8 mile (one way). Rigorous trail.
> **Elevation Change:** 350 feet to 750 feet.
> **Trailhead:** On Brooks Falls Overlook Trail (after 0.5 mile) and on Montara Mountain Trail (after 0.9 mile). The trailheads are well-marked.
> **Wheelchair Accessible:** No.
> **Bench:** No.
> **Bicycles:** No.
> **Horses:** No.
> **Note:** Brooks Creek Trail is the newest trail in the Park. It is narrow and rugged, with an uneven trail surface.

Trail Notes

During the wet winter and spring, Brooks Falls glides down a 175-foot granite fissure on the north slope of Montara Mountain. During the dry summer and fall, only a few rocks glisten moistly. Brooks Creek Trail leads you around the canyon slope opposite the Falls for the closest possible view. Note the nearby sheer granite rockface, an impressive sight any season of the year.

Groves of Manzanita and Golden Chinquapin, Madrones, Willows and dense thickets of Poison Oak grace the slopes along Brooks Creek Trail. Look for Wood Rat nests cascading out onto the trail itself.

For a 2.2-mile loop hike, begin at Montara Mountain Trail trailhead, wind up to Brooks Creek Trail (take either of the two trailheads which are about 500 feet apart), cross downslope to Brooks Falls Overlook Trail and continue to the parking lot.

Wood Rat nest.

Montara Mountain Trail

> **Length:** 2.1 miles (one way). Rigorous trail.
> **Elevation Change:** 200 feet to 1,400 feet.
> **Trailhead:** Near restrooms in Trout Farm Picnic Area.
> **Wheelchair Accessible:** Narrow trail with rocky surface. Switchbacks. Use mountain chairs and the buddy system. Level 1. Extremely difficult.
> **Benches:** Yes.
> **Bicycles:** No.
> **Horses:** Yes.
> **Note:** Montara Mountain Trail connects with Brooks Creek Trail for a loop hike of 2.2 miles.
> Montara Mountain Trail ends at North Peak Access Road in McNee Ranch State Park. Turn uphill to reach North Peak (0.8 mile). Turn downhill to continue to Montara State Beach (2.2 miles).

Trail Notes

Montara Mountain Trail is the most challenging trail in the park. Hike 2.1 miles to the junction with North Peak Access Road in McNee Ranch State Park and continue on, or pause to enjoy the glorious views of Pacifica, San Francisco, the Farallon Islands, Marin County and Point Reyes before returning to San Pedro Valley County Park.

Montara Mountain Trail meets North Peak Access Road at 1,400 feet.

Montara Mountain

Montara Mountain Trail passes through Coastal Scrub and Coastal Chaparral plant communities and through two non-native plant colonies. The lower reaches of the trail wind through a Blue Gum Eucalyptus forest, continually crossing and recrossing a straight row of very old Blue Gums. These were planted in the late 1800s to mark a property line. Offspring of the original trees now cover the hillside, outcompeting native plants.

About a mile and one-half up the trail, note the devastated hilltop overgrown with Pampas Grass. This shameful scar was gouged out in the 1960s by a sportmen's club that later planted the Pampas Grass and Monterey Pines for erosion control. The Pampas Grass has spread to line the old access road, now part of Montara Mountain Trail. Walk around the bulldozed hilltop and note the native plants—Montara Manzanita, Golden Chinquapin, Coyote Bush, Lupine and California Lilac—gaining a slight foothold.

The last half mile of the trail winds across the flank of Montara Mountain in a series of tight switchbacks. As you rest at each turn, enjoy the groves of wind-sheared Montara Manzanita and Golden Chinquapin. Montara Manzanita grows only on Montara Mountain. In the early summer enjoy the feathery banks of Alum Root, the vibrant mounds of Woolly Sunflower and the nodding clumps of Salal.

Building this section of the trail was a challenge met by hard labor and the use of dynamite. Montara Mountain Trail officially opened on October 31, 1990.

Salal

Woolly Sunflower

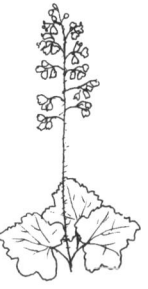

Alum Root

San Pedro Valley County Park

Weiler Ranch Road

Length: 1.0 mile (one-way). Easy trail. Measured jogging trail.
Trailhead: Near Walnut Grove Group Picnic Area.
Wheelchair Accessible: A few slight inclines. Gravel surface. Wide trail. Level 2.
Benches: Yes.
Bicycles: Yes.
Horses: Yes.

Trail Notes

Weiler Ranch Road passes through the narrow, fertile valley of the Middle Fork of San Pedro Creek. Until just a few decades ago, rows of pumpkins, artichokes and other vegetables lined the valley floor, and cattle grazed on the northern slopes. Now, grasses—both native and non-native—and Coastal Scrub assert themselves.

On your way to Weiler Ranch Road, take a slight detour to the creekside picnic tables in the Group Picnic Area. Near them the South Fork and Middle Fork of San Pedro Creek merge to flow out of the Park and on to the Pacific Ocean.

Sunny Weiler Ranch Road is the most heavily used trail in the park—and yet you will see more wildlife along the trail than any place else. Mule Deer graze in the meadows; Bobcats hunt for small mammals; Brush Rabbits nibble along the trail's edge; California Quail dash in and out of the underbrush; and Merriam Chipmunks scold from the Coyote Bush. You may even see Gray Fox and Coyotes coming to the creek to drink. Somehow the wildlife coexists with the walkers, the joggers and the bicyclists.

A Bobcat in hunting position

Montara Mountain

Valley View Trail

Length: 1.4 miles (one way). Moderate trail.
Elevation Change: 200 feet to 550 feet.
Trailhead: On Weiler Ranch Road.
Wheelchair Accessible: Narrow and rigorous with switchbacks. Use mountain chairs and the buddy system. Level 1. Extremely difficult.
Bench: On Weiler Ranch Road.
Bicycles: No.
Horses: Yes.
Note: Valley View Trail and Weiler Ranch Road make a delightful 2-mile loop hike.

Trail Notes

Valley View Trail gently winds to 550 feet from the first trailhead on Weiler Ranch Road and then descends in a series of switchbacks to the second trailhead. Enjoy views of the valley of the Middle Fork of San Pedro Creek and of the Hazelnut Trail switchbacks along Big Canyon across the valley. On clear days, you can see the switchbacks of the upper reaches of Montara Mountain Trail.

Valley View Trail crosses a grassy hillside once used for cattle grazing. Now Coastal Scrub is colonizing the slopes. In the spring, watch the Rattlesnake Grass billow in the wind.

At the highest elevation on Valley View Trail, an unfinished trail beckons you even higher. Eventually this proposed trail will take you to Sweeney Ridge. For the present, consider the trail closed. A few years ago, a hiker took it and soon discovered himself lost in thick Coastal Scrub. Nearly one hundred people and fifteen government agencies spent many long, tense hours searching for him. The story had a happy ending: The hiker was rescued. But it serves as a warning: If you are on Valley View Trail and find yourself on a path that peters out, retrace your steps to the main trail.

Rattlesnake Grass

San Pedro Valley County Park

Hazelnut Trail

> **Length:** 3.7 miles (one way). Rigorous trail.
> **Elevation Change:** 200 feet to 1,000 feet.
> **Trailhead:** On Plaskon Nature Trail and on Weiler Ranch Road.
> **Wheelchair Accessible:** Rigorous trail with many switchbacks. Use mountain chairs and the buddy system. Level 1. Extremely difficult.
> **Benches:** Benches midway on both slopes and at crest.
> **Bicycles:** No.
> **Horses:** Yes.

Trail Notes

Hazelnut Trail is THE plant trail. Nearly every plant on Montara Mountain can be found along its edges: Hazelnut, Creambush, Coffee Berry and Coyote Bush grow at elevations from 200 feet to 1,000 feet; Blue Elderberry, Red Elderberry, Alum Root and Thimbleberry cluster in the lush, damp dells; groves of Manzanita appear above 500 feet; Pacific Starflower carpets the Blue Gum Eucalyptus forest; fragrant California Lilac lines the upper trail; and Huckleberry surrounds the bench at the crest. Trees to watch for are Coast Live Oak, Toyon, Madrone, Coast Silktassel and Golden Chinquapin. Spring flowers include Mission Bells, Fat Solomon's Seal, Slim Solomon's Seal, Douglas Iris and Milkwort.

Hazelnut Trail links the valley of the South Fork of San Pedro Creek to the valley of the Middle Fork, crossing the 1,000-foothigh ridge which separates them. From the bench at the crest, enjoy views of Montara Mountain, Sweeney Ridge, the Pacific Ocean—and a Wood Rat nest. To your left, watch sea gulls commute between Pacifica State Beach in Linda Mar and Pilarcitos Lake, a mile further inland. Perhaps you will see Red-tailed Hawks and Vultures ride the thermals along the ridge you have just climbed.

The trail makes twenty sharp switchbacks along the rim of Big Canyon, which opens into the valley of the Middle Fork. That's quite an awesome accomplishment in trail design.

> If you are a good hiker and if you want to experience the best that San Pedro Valley County Park has to offer—take a hike on the Hazelnut Trail.

San Pedro Valley Then and Now

Fertile, well-watered and sunny San Pedro Valley helped feed the people of San Francisco from 1786 until 1953. The first farmers were the Spanish Mission fathers, who along with Native American Costanos, grew the crops which fed San Francisco's Mission Dolores. The last farmers were Italian–American and Mexican–American artichoke and pea growers, who in the early 1950s, sold their farms to Andrew Oddstad, the builder of the Linda Mar district of Pacifica.

For thousands of years prior to 1786, the Costanos lived in San Pedro Valley, hunting game in the hills, gathering shellfish along the rocky coast, and harvesting hazelnuts, huckleberries and grass seeds from the slopes. Then, early in November of 1769, a Spanish exploring party led by Gaspar de Portolá entered the valley. Portolá and his men had marched north from San Diego, looking for Monterey Bay, which they completely missed. On November 4, they climbed one more ridge—Sweeney Ridge, the northeastern rim of San Pedro Valley—and beheld San Francisco Bay. Today a plaque marks the site, which is part of the Golden Gate National Recreation Area.

> **Portolá Discovery Site**
> To reach the Discovery Site, take Highway 280 to Sneath Lane in San Bruno. Go west on Sneath Lane, crossing Highway 35 (Skyline Boulevard). On your right after about one-half mile, note the San Francisco County Jail, with its herd of buffalo—some alive and some as wooden cut-outs. Continue to the end of the road and park. Walk 1.9 miles uphill on an asphalt road. Turn south (left) at the ridge top to reach the Discovery Site plaque. Turn north (right) to view an old NIKE missile site.
>
> Or, in Pacifica, park at Shelldance Nursery, 2000 Cabrillo Highway (east side of Highway One, north of the Vallemar district). A sign indicates the trailhead for the 2.5-mile hike up Mori Ridge via the NIKE missile site to the Discovery Site.

The Spanish Mission fathers who followed Portolá couldn't grow the food they needed in windy, foggy San Francisco. But they remembered sunny San Pedro Valley, and in 1786 set up an agricultural outpost there.

San Pedro Valley County Park

When the government of Mexico replaced the government of Spain in 1821, the old mission lands were granted to Mexican citizens. Francisco Sanchez got the 8,926 acres known then as Rancho San Pedro and now as the City of Pacifica. Sanchez, a cattle rancher, built his home, the Sanchez Adobe, in San Pedro Valley.

> **Sanchez Adobe**
> The Sanchez Adobe, owned by San Mateo County, is at 1000 Linda Mar Boulevard. Hours are Tuesdays, Wednesdays and Thursdays, 10 AM to 4 PM; Saturdays and Sundays (except holidays), 1 PM to 5 PM. Docent tours. Free admission. (415) 359-1462

In the 1860s, Americans divided up San Pedro Valley into smaller and smaller farms. Irish immigrants grew potatoes and cabbages; Italian immigrants introduced irrigation and planted artichokes and other vegetables. From 1907 through 1920, the farmers shipped their superb San Pedro Valley produce to San Francisco via the Ocean Shore Railroad, which ran along the ocean edge of the valley.

In 1953, suburbia arrived in San Pedro Valley. Hundreds of houses and winding streets replaced the fields of vegetables which once helped feed San Francisco. One hundred and sixty-seven years of farming was virtually over.

San Mateo County began buying the land for San Pedro Valley County Park in the early 1960s. The Visitor Center opened in 1983. Each year over 100,000 people visit this magnificent park at the head of San Pedro Valley.

> **Names**
> The Spanish Mission fathers named their agricultural outpost *San Pedro y San Pablo.* Over time, the surrounding natural features took on the shortened version of the name: San Pedro Valley (sometimes Pedro Valley), San Pedro Creek, and San Pedro Mountain (or Pedro Mountain). Pedro Point shows up as Point San Pedro on some maps.
>
> It's your choice whether you say "Peedro" or "Paydro"—folks use both pronunciations.

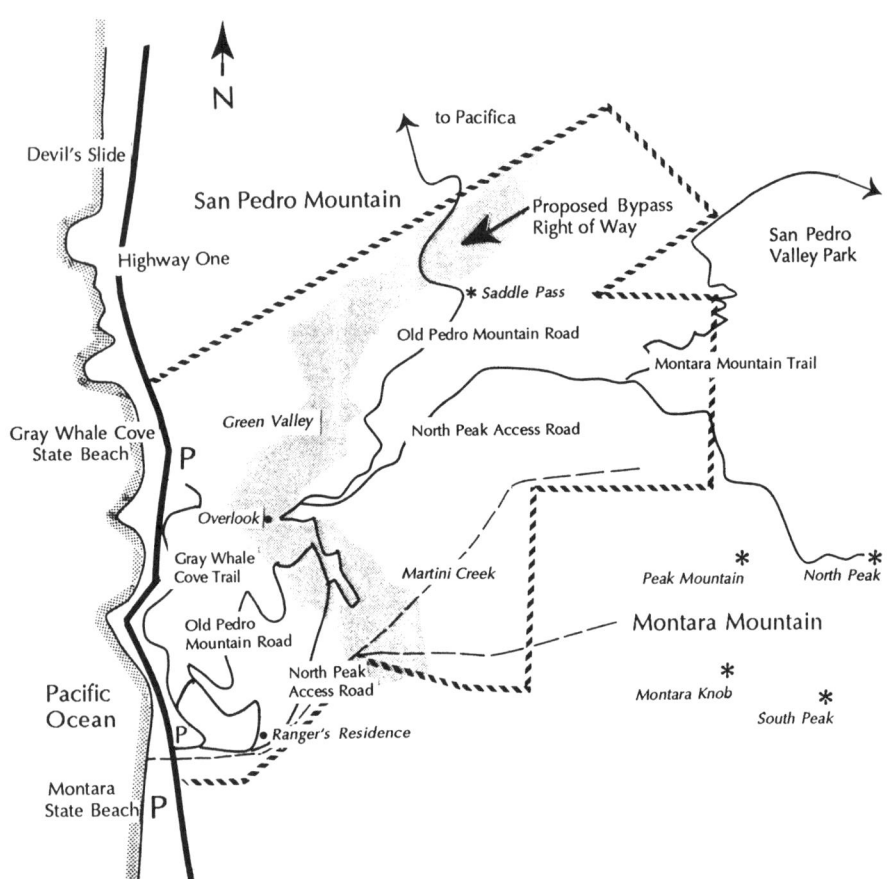

McNee Ranch State Park Trails

Gray Whale Cove Trail: 1 mile one way. Moderate.
Old Pedro Mountain Road: 3.2 miles one way. Rigorous.
North Peak Access Road: 3.9 miles one way. Rigorous.

Wear sturdy shoes, carry water and a jacket. The weather changes rapidly on Montara Mountain. Fierce, chilling winds and dense, dripping fogs are common.

McNee Ranch State Park is undergoing trail development. Please stay on the signed trails and stay off the make-shift trails, which erode the hillsides.

—4—

McNee Ranch State Park

McNee Ranch State Park, on the southern flank of Montara Mountain, offers hikers, bicycle riders and horseback riders magnificent views of the Pacific Ocean and the San Mateo County coast. From the park, you can reach North Peak, the highest point on Montara Mountain (elevation 1,898 feet). If you make it to the top—and there is no fog—the view of the Bay Area, spread below your feet, will take your breath away. Where else can you scan from the Campanile at U. C. Berkeley to Hoover Tower at Stanford University, from Mount Diablo to Mount Tamalpais, from the Pacific Ocean to San Francisco Bay, and from Point Reyes to Pescadero Point?

Within the boundaries of McNee Ranch State Park, you can trace all the human crossings of Montara Mountain, from a Native American Costano trail to the Ocean Shore Railroad to present-day Highway One. You can explore World War II bunkers and contemplate other World War II military installations from afar. You can imagine an old mushroom farm in Green Valley and an old dairy ranch on Martini Creek.

All trails lead through Montara Mountain Coastal Scrub and Coastal Chaparral plant communities. Here you can observe plant associations found nowhere else on earth.

McNee Ranch State Park shares a boundary with San Pedro Valley County Park. A good day hike (4.3 miles one way) begins on the north flank of Montara Mountain in San Pedro Valley County Park and ends on the south flank at Montara State Beach.

Beach Strawberry

McNee Ranch State Park

Where: East side of Highway One between Pacifica and Montara. The park has two entrances: one at Gray Whale Cove State Beach and the other at Martini Creek (near Montara State Beach).

Parking: Free parking at Gray Whale Cove State Beach on the inland side of Highway One, 3 miles south of the Highway One / Linda Mar Boulevard intersection in Pacifica and 1.4 miles north of the Chart House Restaurant in Montara.

Free parking at Montara State Beach on the ocean side of Highway One, 4 miles south of the Linda Mar intersection in Pacifica and 0.4 mile north of the Chart House Restaurant in Montara. To reach the Martini Creek entrance to the park, walk north from the parking lot along the highway for 0.2 mile, then carefully cross the highway.

Limited parking (three to four cars only) is available at the Martini Creek entrance to the park. Do not block the access road.

Telephone: (415) 726-8819 (San Mateo Coast District of the California Department of Parks and Recreation, Half Moon Bay)

Hours: 8 AM to sunset.

Admission Charge: None.

Hiking Trails: Moderate to Rigorous.

Wheelchair Accessible: Trails not rated.

Bicycles: All trails.

Horses: All trails.

Drinking Water: No.

Restrooms: No.

Picnic Tables: Old Pedro Mountain Road at old quarry near Ranger's residence.

Benches: Yes.

Dogs: Yes, on leash.

Fishing: No.

McNee Ranch State Park Volunteers: Meet for trail maintenance at the Ranger's residence on Martini Creek on the last Saturday of every month. Call (415) 726-8819.

Gray Whale Cove State Beach: Clothing optional beach. Entrance fee: $5.00. Gray Whale Cove is a leased concession, not run by the State. Call (415) 728-5336.

McNee Ranch State Park

Gray Whale Cove Trail

Length: 1 mile (one way). Moderate trail.
Elevation Change: 100 feet to 250 feet.
Trailhead: At south end of Gray Whale Cove State Beach parking lot and at Martini Creek park entrance.
Parking: Gray Whale Cove State Beach parking lot, Montara State Beach parking lot, Martini Creek park entrance (three to four cars only).
Benches: Yes.
Bicycles: Yes. Park at Gray Whale Cove State Beach.
Horses: Yes. Park at Gray Whale Cove State Beach.
Note: Gray Whale Cove Trail connects with Old Pedro Mountain Road.

Trail Notes

Take Gray Whale Cove Trail if you want to hike along the edge of the continent. Nothing lies between you and the Pacific Ocean except Highway One on the ledge below.

The trail is fairly flat once you climb the gentle slopes to reach it. From the Martini Creek park entrance, walk around the locked gate to follow the well-marked trail, which parallels the access road. Pass a secluded meadow, climb a hill, and then behold to the south the golden stretch of Montara State Beach and to the north the granite face of Montara Mountain meeting the Pacific Ocean.

From Gray Whale Cove State Beach parking lot (south end), wind around a switchback into a lush dell before coming out on the windswept bluff overhanging Highway One.

You can experience a chain of micro-climates along Gray Whale Cove Trail. First come the windy, grassy ocean bluffs with these ground-hugging wildflowers—

- ❏ Sea Pink
- ❏ Bluff Lettuce
- ❏ Gum Plant
- ❏ Douglas Iris
- ❏ Coast Sun Cup
- ❏ Beach Strawberry
- ❏ Blue Dicks
- ❏ California Buttercup
- ❏ Seaside Daisy
- ❏ Coast Buckwheat
- ❏ Soap Plant
- ❏ Wild Hollyhock
- ❏ Coast Paintbrush
- ❏ Varicolored Lupine
- ❏ Blue-eyed Grass
- ❏ Farewell-to-Spring

Montara Mountain

Then, the trail dips inland to moist dells overgrown with these Coastal Scrub plants—

- ❑ Coyote Bush
- ❑ California Blackberry
- ❑ Sticky Money Flower
- ❑ California Bee Plant
- ❑ Cow Parsnip
- ❑ Coast Sagebrush
- ❑ Poison Oak
- ❑ Lizard Tail
- ❑ Coffee Berry
- ❑ Henderson's Angelica

Dwarf Coyote Bush, spread like a mat, surrounds the bench above the Martini Creek park entrance.

Coast Sun Cup

Seaside Daisy

Birds are common along Gray Whale Cove Trail. Watch for Red-tailed Hawks, Bewick's Wrens, Wrentits, Rufous-sided Towhees, White-crowned Sparrows and Scrub Jays.

From December through March, you might see California Gray Whales migrating offshore. Look for water spouts and flashing slivers of gray-black backs as the whales submerge and resurface. As many as 15,000 Gray Whales swim past Devil's Slide on their journey from the Bering Sea to Baja California. January is the peak month for southbound Gray Whales; March the peak month for northbound whales.

Green Valley

At Gray Whale Cove State Beach parking lot, take a few minutes to hike up to the locked yellow gate which stretches across a road cut through a small hill. Green Valley lies just ahead. (The road beyond the gate is closed to the public.) The cut was blasted out by the engineers of the Ocean Shore Railroad, which ran along the San Mateo County coast from 1907 through 1920. You are standing in the middle of the old Ocean Shore roadbed: The whistle of hundreds of puffing, oil-fired locomotives once echoed off these granite walls. The Highway One cut just oceanward was blasted out in 1937. The route of the railroad and the highway merge at the parking lot and head south together. Like all road cuts on Montara Mountain, these are lined with invasive Pampas Grass.

McNee Ranch State Park

At Gray Whale Cove parking lot, you can see the cut used by the Ocean Shore Railroad (to the right) and the cut Highway One uses (to the left). San Pedro Mountain is in the distance. In the wet winter of 1982, Caltrans temporarily routed Highway One through the parking lot (along the asphalt strip) while it rebuilt washed-out Highway One.

Until fairly recently, Green Valley was used for agriculture and cattle grazing. The ranch house at the head of the valley—best seen from Old Pedro Mountain Road—dates from before World War II. In the late 1940s, the rancher grew mushrooms in four mushroom houses. Now Coastal Scrub vegetation has asserted itself.

In the late 1960s, lovely Green Valley almost became the San Mateo County dump. The land was owned by Henry Doelger, who also owned much of the Coastside. Doelger built the Sunset District of San Francisco and the Westlake District of Daly City, and he had similar plans for the land south of Montara Mountain. Coastsiders unanimously rallied against the proposed dump, and the County dropped the idea. Doelger built only one subdivision on the Coastside—Clipper Ridge north of El Granada.

On the promontory to the north of Gray Whale Cove is an old World War II bunker, standing like a sentry on a column of rock. The bunker was a base-end station, staffed by soldiers who sighted offshore targets, pinpointed their locations, and telephoned the information to artillery batteries north and south of the Golden Gate. In the 1970s, a developer, planning to build an estate, shaved off the promontory around the bunker. His plans fell through—and the bunker stands as a lonely monument to the World War II coastal defenses along the San Mateo County coast. The promontory is off-limits for hiking.

Montara Mountain

Relatively flat Gray Whale Cove Trail is part of what was once the main road—from 1879 until 1915—between San Francisco and the town of Half Moon Bay. The rest of the Half Moon Bay–Colma Road was not so level. North from Green Valley the road wound to the top of Devil's Slide and then steeply dropped to the valley of Shamrock Ranch in the Linda Mar district of Pacifica. You can still see bits and pieces of the old road, now flagged by Pampas Grass.

Highway One, running like a shadow just below Gray Whale Cove Trail, uses the old Ocean Shore Railroad roadbed between Gray Whale Cove State Beach and Montara State Beach. In the early 1900s, horses trotted along the highroad, while Ocean Shore trains puffed along the low road.

Names
In the mid-1800s, Green Valley was known as Cañada Verde. As an Ocean Shore Railroad water-stop, it was Green Canyon. Now everyone says Green Valley.

Coastsiders called Gray Whale Cove "Match Box Cove" until the 1960s, when the owner changed the name to honor the Gray Whales passing along its shore. Earlier cove residents had passionately collected matchbox covers to line the walls of their house on the ledge above the beach—hence the name.

McNee Ranch State Park

Old Pedro Mountain Road

Length: 3.2 miles (one way). Rigorous trail.
Elevation Change: 100 feet to 922 feet.
Trailhead: Martini Creek park entrance.
Parking: Montara State Beach parking lot and Martini Creek park entrance (three to four cars only).
Bicycles: Yes.
Horses: Yes.
Benches: Yes.
Picnic Tables: At old quarry near Ranger's residence.
Note: Old Pedro Mountain Road, an asphalt road, connects several times with North Peak Access Road, a dirt road. If you want to reach the Saddle Pass, stay on the asphalt road. If you decide to go to North Peak, follow the dirt road.

Trail Notes

Enter McNee Ranch State Park at the Martini Creek park entrance and follow the access road for 0.2 mile to the Ranger's residence.

The Martini Creek entrance to McNee Ranch State Park. Gray Whale Cove Trail is to the left; the access road to the right. Two of Montara Mountain's four peaks are in the distance: Peak Mountain on the left and South Peak on the right.

Montara Mountain

Martini Creek, which drains a large part of Montara Mountain, flows in the deep gorge alongside the access road. Across the creek is a field of cultivated Lily-of-the-Nile. The old Monterey Pine, Monterey Cypress and Blue Gum Eucalyptus trees indicate ranchers have lived at the end of the access road for a long time. The Ranger's residence itself dates from the 1930s. The Martinis, for whom the creek is named, farmed this section of the Coastside in the early 1900s. Some of their fence posts still line Gray Whale Cove Trail.

Turn left at the fork in the road before the Ranger's residence. Here begins your hike to the Saddle Pass (elevation 922 feet) along Old Pedro Mountain Road. Note the yellow Montara granite in the old quarry and along the road cuts ahead. The magnificent clean yellow sand of Montara State Beach begins here on the southern flanks of Montara Mountain and then washes down Martini Creek to the shore.

Old Pedro Mountain Road passes through typical Coastal Scrub—Coyote Bush, Coffee Berry, Coast Sagebrush and Poison Oak. Non-native colonizers—Monterey Pine, Monterey Cypress, Pampas Grass and Acacia—line the lower reaches of the trail.

Gray Whale Cove Overlook. The town of Montara is in the distance.

About halfway up the trail, you come out at Gray Whale Cove Overlook, which offers stunning views of the coastline. Continue on the asphalt road about 0.1 mile to the overgrown path marked by wooden utility poles, which leads down the side of Green Valley. If you feel up to trail blazing and can handle Poison Oak, follow the steep path down to two World War II concrete bunkers. Look for the air vent pipe coming up from the tunnel which connects the two bunkers. Further on are concrete antenna foundations. No one seems

McNee Ranch State Park

to remember the precise function of these bunkers. The best guess is that they housed electronic aircraft tracking equipment. The Army planted the iceplant that still grows around the bunkers for camouflage. Sight across Green Valley to the World War II emplacements on top of the promontory at Devil's Slide and to the elevated bunker on the promontory at Gray Whale Cove. These three sites remind us of World War II on the San Mateo County coast.

World War II concrete bunker nearly overgrown by Coastal Scrub above Green Valley just off Old Pedro Mountain Road.

To continue to the Saddle Pass, stay on the asphalt road. The dirt road takes you to North Peak. Note the white plastic irrigation pipes leading to dead plants along sections of the road. Caltrans attempted to replant Coastal Scrub after taking soil samples for the proposed Devil's Slide Bypass, which would cross the mountain here.

McNee Ranch State Park ends just beyond the Saddle Pass. At the Saddle, enjoy views of Pacifica, San Francisco and Marin County. Old Pedro Mountain Road winds down into Pacifica, coming out on Higgins Way. The Saddle Pass can be extremely foggy, with the wind howling in the power lines overhead.

Old Pedro Mountain Road was built in 1915 by the County of San Mateo. Then, it was called the Coastside Boulevard and served as the main road between San Francisco and Half Moon Bay. In 1937, when Highway One along Devil's Slide opened, motorists took the easier route. After World War II, Old Pedro Mountain Road was closed to traffic. As you hike the old road, imagine what a challenge it must have been to drive. Oldtimers remember throwing up in the back seats of their parents' cars as they wound their way over the mountain.

Park Rangers have counted at least 16 dumped cars in the park. Look for the old car buried under a Wood Rat nest at the head of Green Valley far below the trail.

North Peak Access Road

Length: 3.9 miles (one way). Rigorous trail.
Elevation Change: 100 feet to 1,898 feet.
Trailhead: Martini Creek park entrance.
Parking: Montara State Beach and Martini Creek park entrance (three to four cars only).
Bicycles: Yes.
Horses: Yes.
Bench: No.

Trail Notes

Enter McNee Ranch State Park at the Martini Creek park entrance and stay on the access road. Take the right fork at the Ranger's residence. Note the old cement-block barn across the creek. Once it was a slaughter house. Now it is a private horse stable. The concrete bridge foundations for Old Pedro Mountain Road, which crossed the creek here, are still visible. Martini Creek offers excellent bird watching.

Continue on North Peak Access Road (very steep) for 0.6 mile to Old Pedro Mountain Road. The Coastal Scrub is barely waist-high on this dry south slope. The two trails continue together until above Green Valley. If you are tired of climbing, take the asphalt Old Pedro Mountain Road to the Saddle Pass (elevation change 200 feet in about one mile). If you want an exhilarating hike (elevation change 1,100 feet in about two miles), take the dirt road to North Peak, the top of Montara Mountain.

North Peak Access Road leads you along a ridge, sometimes giving you views to the Golden Gate and beyond, other times views of the Coastside. Listen for Wrentits, whose song sounds like a ping-pong ball bouncing on a tabletop, as you circle the canyon drained by Martini Creek.

Wrentit

McNee Ranch State Park

The junction with Montara Mountain Trail, which descends to San Pedro Valley County Park, is marked by a wooden retaining wall. (No bicycles allowed on Montara Mountain Trail.) You are standing above Brooks Falls and part of the San Pedro Creek watershed. Moisture-loving Thimbleberry, California Lilac, Creambush and Hazelnut dominate these high dells, and Western Bleeding Heart grows along the trail. The presence of Manzanita and Golden Chinquapin indicates that this is Coastal Chaparral.

Continue on to the high meadow bound by four peaks: North Peak, Peak Mountain, Montara Knob and South Peak. In the spring, masses of Sea Pink interspersed with Common Wallflower fill the meadow. The trail leads directly to antenna-covered North Peak. Sit below the antennas on the highest rock, and if you are lucky and it is a clear day, you will see the Bay Area spread out at your feet. The vast open space directly below you, including Pilarcitos Lake, is San Francisco's Peninsula Watershed. It is off-limits for hiking. To the northeast lie the switchbacks of Hazelnut Trail in San Pedro Valley County Park. In June, you cannot help noticing the Cobweb Thistle. North Peak (elevation 1,898 feet) has a well-scratched triangulation marker labelled "Soupy."

North Peak is private property (public use allowed). PG&E, San Mateo County and other agencies lease the communication towers.

North Peak Access Road.

> Wear good gripping footwear for a hike on North Peak Access Road. The grainy trail surface makes the descent similar to walking on ball-bearings. Take warm windbreakers: The weather changes rapidly on North Peak. Howling winds and dense, dripping fogs are common.

49

Montara Mountain

Communication towers on North Peak. Peak Mountain is in the distance.

Climb Peak Mountain (elevation 1,827 feet) to add a pebble to the growing cairn started by an El Granada resident. Note the triangulation marker labelled "Pedro."

South Peak (elevation 1,846 feet) and Montara Knob (elevation 1,646 feet) are off-limits for hiking. South Peak is nearly due south from North Peak. Montara Knob, on the same ridge as South Peak, looks like a dark green cone.

Pacifica, San Francisco and Marin County from North Peak.

McNee Ranch State Park Then and Now

McNee Ranch was a very small part of Duncan McNee's empire. When McNee died in Oakland in 1913, newspapers extolled him as "an early California land baron." At one time, he owned 800,000 acres in California, plus mineral rights to 14,000 acres in nineteen counties.

Duncan McNee was born in Canada in 1849 and came to San Francisco in 1864. He started out as a clerk in the U. S. Land Office, then opened a dredging business to dredge San Francisco Bay. Next, he invested in mines, in oil fields and in timberlands all over the West.

McNee Company, which survived McNee, sold off its last California land holdings in 1964.

The land of McNee Ranch, from Spanish and Mexican times until recently, was always used for cattle grazing. American ranchers also grew grain and hay on the slopes. In the 1950s, it was part of a dairy ranch.

During World War II, the U. S. Army commandeered McNee Ranch. First, soldiers built bunkers above Green Valley. Next, the Army decided to use the isolated ranch for commando training. Coastsiders were warned off the slopes and off Old Pedro Mountain Road: The commandos used live ammunition.

In the late 1970s, the State of California bought the 625-acre McNee Ranch from Half Moon Bay Properties for one million dollars. McNee Ranch State Park officially opened in 1984.

> **McNee Ranch State Park versus the Devil's Slide Bypass**
> The integrity of McNee Ranch State Park—and Montara Mountain—is at stake. The proposed Devil's Slide Bypass, which involves massive cuts and fills, would bisect the park, disrupt plant and animal habitats, and change the current trail system. Green Valley would be scoured out just below Old Pedro Mountain Road for the three-lane Bypass. The World War II bunkers would be bulldozed under.
>
> Today, enjoy the serene trails through Coastal Scrub, thank the Park Volunteers who maintain them, and hope that the proposed Bypass will never disrupt McNee Ranch State Park.
>
> **Hands Across Montara Mountain:** On May 1, 1994, people who love Montara Mountain joined hands at the Saddle Pass in protest against the proposed Devil's Slide Bypass.

Montara Mountain

Reflections

A Hike on Montara Mountain
by Madge Morris Wagner

Madge Morris Wagner and her family—Mr. Commuter, daughter "Huwa" and three other children—lived in Moss Beach during the Ocean Shore Railroad years. In 1913 they enjoyed this outing on Montara Mountain.

After skirting to the left, another and a taller peak was ascended—Peak Mountain.

"That's the top, up there," said Mr. C., indicating a rocky place above his head.

"It doesn't look like a top to me—it's too flat," said his wife, clinging to the precipitous mountain-side some yards below.

"It may be a table-top," said Mr. C.

"Well, if it is, when we get there, let's eat," said his wife.

But when they got there, they found it was only the first of several terraces, and there was much zigzagging, and planting of heels and toes in gopher and snake holes for a footing before the real top was reached.

Of course, Mr. C. reached the top first, and then "Huwa," who looked as if about to be blown off, so strong was the wind.

What a sublime view they beheld!

From Farallone–Montara Beach to Half Moon Bay was practically one great valley, with little valleys opening into it—an ideal site for a large city like Oakland.

Moss Beach, Farallone and Montara were clearly discernible, with their cypress hedges, and a glimpse of their beaches. The eye followed down Seal Cove to Marine View, where Groskurth's Hotel, Mr. Commuter declared, looked like a ten-story office building. Pillar Point and Princeton were in plain sight, and also the green fields through which an Ocean Shore train was speeding.

Within this valley, surrounded by the ocean with its cliffs and bays on three sides, and by the mountains on the other, could be found a beautiful location for a great college, a sanitarium, magnificent country homes, and a site for a complete and ideal American City.

They turned around and looked down the other side of the peak. There lay a beautiful fertile little valley opening onto the beach at Tobin [San Pedro Valley], and more mountains.

After writing their names on a paper drinking-cup and leaving it under a stone on the tip-top, where any readers of the *Coast Side Comet* may find them, the Commuter and his party dropped down into a declivity, and climbed up the other side of another peak, which looked to be the tallest of the three high ones. This was North Peak.

"Huwa" was the first to reach the summit. There to the east, past fold after fold of mountains, could be seen the sheen of San Francisco Bay, and the Commuters saw what Portolá saw and more.

Fog obscured the city proper, but a rift disclosed blue Tamalpais Mountains. The town of South San Francisco lay clear in the sunlight.

Across the Bay, the hills stood out, and beyond to the northeast, Mt. Diablo. San Mateo Point and the Dumbarton cut-off distinguished the south end of the Bay.

From this windy summit could be seen, in all its beauty, the San Pedro Valley, and beyond in the ocean, Mussel Rock.

After adding three more stones to the summit to make it higher, the Commuter and his companions crawled down on the southern slope to get out of the wind.

Beneath in the valley, like a snake, wound the road; and toward the southeast lay a blue arm of Pilarcitos Lake, one of the chain of Spring Valley Lakes, from which comes San Francisco's water supply.

Scarper Peak beckoned to the travellers from the south. The Commuter spread out his maps and studied them, while his wife and daughter studied the landscape. They could see redwood covered mountains, indicating Big Basin; the little town of Half Moon Bay lying in the sunlight by its Bay; and beyond, the point at San Gregorio. They could see even as far as Pescadero.

"It is about four miles in a bee line to Moss Beach," the Commuter said, "but five or six to walk."

While eating their lunch, they looked down and could see where the headwaters of San Vicente Creek arise, to flow down between Moss Beach and Seal Cove to the sea.

They proceeded down one slope and up another, which brought them to the top of South Peak.

A hogback route was picked out for the return [to Moss Beach].
—condensed from August 8 and August 15, 1913 *Coast Side Comet*

A Quick Guide to Coastal Scrub and Coastal Chaparral on Montara Mountain

Elevation: Coastal Scrub at lower elevations. Coastal Chaparral above 500 feet.

Environment: Foggy, with harsh, salt-laden winds near the ocean. Dry summers, wet winters. Shady, damp, north-facing slopes are lusher than dry, sunny, south-facing slopes.

Overall appearance: Dominated by shrubs.

Coastal Scrub Indicator Plants: Coyote Bush, Coast Sagebrush, Sticky Monkey Flower, Coast Paintbrush, Seaside Daisy, Coast Buckwheat.

Coastal Chaparral Indicator Plants: California Lilac, Yerba Santa, Manzanita, Coffee Berry, Golden Chinquapin.

Common characteristic of plants: Conserve moisture during dry summers by having leathery leaves, light green leaves, small leaves, leaves that curl under, hairy leaves, or waxy leaves.

Blooming Season: Nearly year around beginning with Manzanita in January and ending with Coyote Bush in October–December.

Manzanita

Coyote Bush

~5~

Plants on Montara Mountain

Montara Mountain is unique. The complex and diverse Coastal Scrub and Coastal Chaparral plant communities in its valleys and on its slopes are found nowhere else on earth. No place else has the same plants, soils, and exposures as does Montara Mountain. No place else has groves of Montara Manzanita and Golden Chinquapin on the higher slopes, an intricate Hazelnut–Sword Fern plant community on the northern slopes, and masses of spring wildflowers on the ocean bluffs.

Montara Mountain is a virtually untouched—and unstudied— California native plant island amidst the six million people of the San Francisco Bay Area. For these people and for the generations to come, Montara Mountain is a resource which must be treated gently and with respect.

From Grasslands to Coastal Scrub

Montara Mountain has not always offered such a complex and diverse botanical feast. When the Spanish explored Montara Mountain in 1769, they found an "extremely high range of hills, steep and cliffy on all sides, all bare and treeless with nothing but ground and grass, and a great deal of brambles."[1]

When a botanist sailed between Santa Cruz and San Francisco in 1846, he noted that "The whole of the coast is destitute of trees or shrubs, with the exception of Point Año Nuevo."[2]

---

[1] Stanger and Brown, p. 96.
[2] Gordon, p. 129.

Montara Mountain

Why is our Montara Mountain so much more diverse than the Montara Mountain of yesteryear?

The explanation begins with the Native American Costanos. By using fire as a tool, the Costanos limited the diversity of plant life on Montara Mountain. Every fall for thousands of years they burned the San Mateo County coast. Their skillfully set fires raged over the hillsides and coastal terraces, consuming dry grasses and any pioneer seedlings of Coastal Scrub plants. By burning the coast, the Costanos assured themselves of a good crop of grass seeds—an important part of their diet—the following summer.

The grassy valleys and slopes appealed to the Spanish and Mexican ranchers who came next. Their longhorn cattle thrived on the nutritious native bunch grasses and on the alien grasses, such as Wild Oats, which the ranchers brought with them. In 1827, one traveller wrote, "A fine verdure clothed the plains and hills where we now saw continually immense herds of cattle, sheep and horses. The land between San Francisco and Monterey is nothing but one continuous pasture."[3]

American ranchers, who arrived on the San Mateo County coast in the 1850s, continued to graze cattle, but they also grew grain and hay in the valleys and on the slopes. In the early 1900s, the ranchers became farmers and concentrated on growing vegetables, such as artichokes and Brussels sprouts, in the flatlands. Hillside fields were abandoned and Coastal Scrub—after millennia of Native American fires and decades of Spanish, Mexican and American cattle grazing—began to assert itself.

In the 1950s, when suburbia found its way to the San Mateo County coast, farmers abandoned more fields. Coastal Scrub advanced even further along the undeveloped slopes and coastal terraces.

Today, Coastal Scrub is still colonizing Montara Mountain. Note Coyote Bush, California Blackberry and Coast Sagebrush in the abandoned grassy fields in San Pedro Valley County Park along Valley View Trail, and in McNee Ranch State Park along Gray Whale Cove Trail and lower North Peak Access Road. Eventually these slopes will display the rich diversity of Coastal Scrub.

---

[3]Burcham, p. 98.

A Who's Who of Colonizers

The First Wave of Colonizers
Non-native annuals colonize abandoned fields first. They are fast growing and produce a lot of seeds and offspring, which build up the soil for the native shrubs and perennials that follow. Some first-wave colonizers are:

Wild Radish	Wild Oats
Field Mustard	Poison Hemlock
Sow Thistle	Scarlet Pimpernel

The Second Wave of Colonizers
Coastal Scrub plants—woody bushes and low-growing perennials—quickly follow the non-natives. Some second-wave colonizers are:

Coyote Bush	Yarrow
Coffee Berry	Pearly Everlasting
Coast Sagebrush	Coast Buckwheat
Lizard Tail	Bluff Lettuce
Poison Oak	Coast Paintbrush
California Blackberry	California Poppy
California Bee Plant	Yerba Santa
Sticky Monkey Flower	Henderson's Angelica
Bush Lupine	Thimbleberry
Beach Strawberry	Franciscan Paintbrush

Four Non-native Plants

Coastal Scrub is dense. Stand on Old Pedro Mountain Road and visualize pushing your way cross-country through the tangle of Coffee Berry, Coyote Bush, Yerba Santa and Poison Oak. A daunting proposition—and you decide to stay on the trail. Now, visualize two fluffy windblown seeds from non-native Pampas Grass. One drifts into the Coastal Scrub, gets hung up on a twig of Coyote Bush and will never germinate. The other drifts over the trail, drops to a bare patch of ground and begins to grow. One more Pampas Grass starts life along a trail on Montara Mountain. Coastal Scrub can keep non-natives out; trails and old road cuts cannot. As you hike Montara Mountain, especially on the southern slopes, you can pick out the old roads simply by following the marching lines of Pampas Grass.

Montara Mountain

Here are four non-natives to watch for along the trails:

Monterey Pine and Monterey Cypress

In the mid-1800s, tree-hungry ranchers planted the first Monterey Pines and Monterey Cypresses along the San Mateo County coast, importing them from the Monterey Peninsula, one hundred miles to the south. Note their offspring near old ranches along San Pedro Creek and Martini Creek. Some offspring have colonized stretches of Old Pedro Mountain Road and the disturbed hillsides on the southern flanks of Montara Mountain.

Blue Gum Eucalyptus

Blue Gum Eucalyptus, native to Australia, has been in California since 1853, when the first seedlings were planted at the tip of the foggy, treeless San Francisco Peninsula. At first, Blue Gum seedlings were so rare they cost between $5 and $10 each. But by the early 1870s, anyone could buy a seedling for a dime, and everyone did. Millions of trees were planted, many on the San Mateo County coast. Some people thought huge groves of Blue Gums would keep disease at bay; others thought Blue Gums would make fine furniture. Still others planted whole hillsides for firewood. But none of their hopes was justified: Blue Gum wood made lousy furniture—it cracked and warped when it dried; people realized that fragrant air didn't cure diseases; and electricity, oil and gas replaced wood for heating. Today, with tens of thousands of acres of Blue Gum Eucalyptus in California, we live with the legacy of turn-of-the-century, dime-a-seedling, get-rich-quick schemes.

In San Pedro Valley County Park, look for a row of Blue Gums along Brooks Creek at the end of Brooks Falls Overlook Trail and in groves along Valley View Trail, Hazelnut Trail and Montara Mountain Trail. Before you enter the groves notice how richly varied the Coastal Scrub is—with shrubs and perennials of all sizes and hues. Once in the groves, note how limited the vegetation is, except for Poison Oak, which thrives in nearly every situation. In Australia, a Blue Gum Eucalyptus grove supports a rich variety of plants, birds, insects and mammals. But not here. Blue Gum leaves, full of oily terpenes, inhibit the seed germination of Coastal Scrub plants. If by chance, a native plant does sprout, the greedy Blue Gums surrounding it will tap most of the soil nutrients and water, ensuring that the native will be a scrawny one.

Blue Gums produce a lot of forest litter, which is extremely flammable, especially during the dry California summers and falls. Blue Gums make trails dangerous for hikers: the seed capsules act like ball bearings, and the leaves are as slick as ice.

Pampas Grass

Two species of Pampas Grass grow in California: the gentle species, *Cortaderia selloana*, and the untamed species, *Cortaderia jubata*. Both have beautiful flowering plumes. The gentle species is infertile; the untamed species is very fertile. Guess which species you see all along the California coast and marching across Montara Mountain.

In the 1850s, horticulturists imported the gentle species from Argentina for its fashionable plumes, which decorated countless turn-of-the-century homes. Fashions changed, and the gentle species, known by flowering plumes no taller than its leaves, languished as an ornamental plant in a few backyards.

In the 1950s, horticulturists imported the untamed species from Bolivia for erosion control. Caltrans planted it on road cuts up and down the coast. But by the 1970s, everyone knew that this species of Pampas Grass was a disaster. Each fertile plume produced thousands of windblown seeds, which quickly sprouted in any disturbed patch of soil they lighted upon. California native plants couldn't compete with the newcomer and soon tens of thousands of flowering plumes, standing high above the narrow leaves, waved from the hillsides along Highway One.

On Montara Mountain, Pampas Grass outcompetes Coyote Bush. Coyote Bush feeds many animals, but no animals feed on the razor-sharp leaves of Pampas Grass. Eradication of Pampas Grass is costly and difficult, involving intensive labor, back hoes and heavy-duty chemicals.

Pampas Grass and Monterey Cypress along Old Pedro Mountain Road.

Plants on Montara Mountain

The plants on Montara Mountain include flowering annuals and perennials, shrubs, trees, ferns and grasses. Use this guide as a quick reference to identify the most common plants and their flowering times. Note that shrubs are included in the flower sections.

Coastal Scrub is at lower elevations near the ocean. Coastal Chaparral is at higher elevations inland.

Plants vary in their growth habits, depending on soil, exposure to wind, rainfall, and whether they grow on north-facing slopes or on south-facing slopes. For example, on damp, sheltered, north-facing slopes, shrubby Coffee Berry can be from six to eight feet tall, with lush, six-inch-long leaves. On dry, windy, south-facing slopes, Coffee Berry is waist-high, with moisture-conserving, rolled-under, three-inch-long leaves.

In the spring, be sure to hike Gray Whale Cove Trail in McNee Ranch State Park and Hazelnut Trail in San Pedro Valley County Park for the best displays of wildflowers on Montara Mountain.

No-bend botany

Trails through hilly terrain offer one advantage to trailside botanists—no-bend botany. The upslope along nearly every trail on Montara Mountain spreads forth a cornucopia of plants to examine without bending over. There before you, at eye level, beckon the intricate flowers of Douglas Iris, Franciscan Paintbrush and Sticky Monkey Flower.

Enjoy!

The Bouquet of Montara Mountain
Be sure to enjoy the fragrances of Montara Mountain. Smell the flowers of California Lilac, Henderson's Angelica and Bush Lupine, and the leaves of Coast Sagebrush, Hedge Nettle, Yerba Buena, Coyote Mint, Pitcher Sage and Mugwort. Some fragrances are more pleasant than others. Taken together, they all are part of the memorable bouquet of Montara Mountain.

White Flowers

Learn to tell Poison Oak from California Blackberry.

Poison Oak
All trails; common.
Sprawling, climbing vine or bushy shrub. Deciduous.
Flowers: Whitish-green, small; in dangling clusters. April–June.
Fruit: Smooth green balls ripening to white; in dangling clusters.
Leaves: Three leaflets per leaf: glossy red-green in spring, shiny green in summer, red in fall.
Note: Be alert when you hike. All parts of Poison Oak—leaves, flowers, fruit, stems—contain toxic oils and cause **severe skin reactions**. Learn to recognize Poison Oak and to tell it from California Blackberry.
Poison Oak has no prickles on leaves and stems; California Blackberry has prickles.
Toxicodendron diversilobum

California Blackberry
All trails; common.
Sprawling and mounding; prickly stems. Deciduous.
Flowers: White, five petals, one inch across. April–July.
Fruit: Red berries ripening to black. July–August.
Leaves: Three leaflets per prickly leaf.
Note: Remember that California Blackberry has prickly leaves and stems. Poison Oak has no prickles.
Himalaya Berry (*Rubus procerus*), also found on Montara Mountain, has five prickly leaflets, white to pinkish-white flowers and black berries.
Rubus ursinus

White Flowers

3, 4, 5, or 6 petals

Coast Trillium / Western Wake Robin
Shady, damp trails. Plaskon Nature Trail.
Six to twelve inches tall.
Flowers: White, turning pink with age, three petals; single flower on two-inch stem above leaves. March.
Leaves: Dark green, large and triangular; three per plant on top of five-inch stem.
Trillium ovatum

White Globe Lily
Rocky outcrops; rare.
One to two feet tall.
Flowers: White, tinged with pink and translucent, three petals, one inch in diameter, globe-shaped; hang from stems. April–June.
Leaves: Long and narrow.
Calochortus albus

Milkmaids
Shady, damp trails; common. Brooks Falls Overlook Trail.
One to two feet tall.
Flowers: White to light pink, four petals; in clusters at tops of stems. February–April.
Leaves: Oval lower leaves and three-part, lance-shaped upper leaves.
Dentaria californica

Field Chickweed
Grassy trails.
Five to ten inches tall; sticky stems.
Flowers: White, five petals with notches, one-half inch across, fragrant. March–May.
Leaves: Light green, one to two inches long; in pairs.
Cerastium arvense

White Flowers

Beach Strawberry
Bluff trails; common. Gray Whale Cove Trail.
Low growing; spreads by bright red runners.
Flowers: White, five petals. March–August.
Fruit: Small and red; hard to see.
Leaves: Made up of three toothed, coarse-looking leaflets.
Fragaria chiloensis

Sticky Cinquefoil
Dry trails; common.
One to three feet tall; slippery stems.
Flowers: White with yellow centers, five petals. March–July.
Leaves: Made up of five to nine coarsely toothed leaflets.
Potentilla glandulosa

Douglas Nightshade
All trails; common.
Two to four feet high; bushy.
Flowers: White to whitish-lavender with yellow centers, five petals, tomato-like; in loose clusters. April–October.
Fruit: Black balls.
Leaves: Triangular, gently lobed; in pairs.
Note: Douglas Nightshade is poisonous.
Solanum douglasii

Soap Plant
All trails; common.
One-half foot to three feet tall.
Flowers: White with green or purple veins, six petals, spidery looking, open up in late afternoon; in loose clusters on branching stems. May–June.
Seeds: In green-black capsules.
Leaves: Wavy, narrow, one foot or more long; in wide spreading circle around base of plant.
Chlorogalum pomeridianum

White Flowers

Wood Orchid
Bluff trails; uncommon.
One to two feet tall; stout stem.
Flowers: Six petals—three white and three green—with long spur, one-half inch across; in dense clusters along stem. August.
Leaves: Small and erect; tightly line stem.
Habenaria elegans

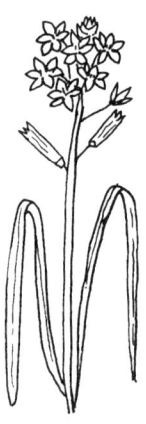

Star Lily
Dry trails. Montara Mountain Trail.
Two to three feet tall; stout stem.
Flowers: White, six petals, star-shaped; in clusters along stem. March–April.
Seeds: In one-to-two-inch upright, lingering pods. May.
Leaves: Narrow and long; at base of stem.
Zigadenus fremontii

Slim Solomon's Seal
Damp slopes along trails; common. Hazelnut Trail.
One to two feet tall; single stem.
Flowers: White, six petals, star-like; in loose clusters along stem. February–April.
Fruit: Red and white striped balls. May–June.
Leaves: Narrow, two to four inches long.
Smilacina stellata var *sessilifolia*

White Flowers

Fat Solomon's Seal
Damp slopes along trails; common. Hazelnut Trail.
One to three feet tall; single stem.
Flowers: White, six petals, tiny; in dense clusters along stem. March–April.
Fruit: Bright red balls; in clusters. June.
Leaves: Three to six inches long, oval with wavy edges.
Smilacina racemosa var *amplexicaulis*

Many Tiny Flowers

Sweet Alyssum
Garden escapee; common. Gray Whale Cove Trail.
Four to six inches tall.
Flowers: White, tiny, numerous, fragrant; in loose domes at ends of stems. April–June.
Seeds: Transparent, eye-glass-like seed pods.
Leaves: Narrow.
Lobularia maritima

Miner's Lettuce
Shady, damp trails; common. Brooks Falls Overlook Trail.
Four to ten inches tall.
Flowers: White and tiny; in clusters above saucer-like leaves. March–May.
Leaves: Narrow and fleshy; at base of stems.
Montia perfoliata

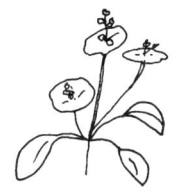

Coast Buckwheat
Rocky slopes along trails; common.
Six inches to two feet tall.
Flowers: Whitish-pink, tiny; in ball-like clusters on top of leafless stems. May–October.
Leaves: Dark green above, white and woolly below, wavy edges; in dense clumps at base of stems.
Eriogonum latifolium

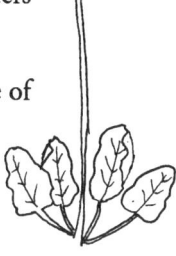

White Flowers

Tiny Flowers in Umbrellas

Pearly Everlasting
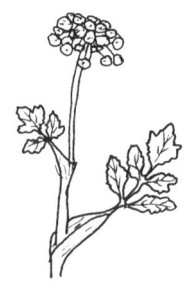
Dry trails; common.
One-half foot to three feet tall.
Flowers: Papery white bracts with yellow flowers in the centers; in tight clusters at tops of stems. June–September.
Leaves: Dark green, narrow, three to four inches long. No fragrance.
Note: Fragrant Everlasting (*Gnaphalium* sp) is in bloom from April–August. Leaves are narrow, gray-green, woolly and very fragrant. Flowers are similar to Pearly Everlasting.
Anaphalis margaritacea

Henderson's Angelica
Damp slopes along bluff trails; common. Gray Whale Cove Trail.
Two to five feet tall; stout stems.
Flowers: White, tiny, numerous, sweet fragrance; clustered in balls to form five-to-six-inch umbrellas. May–July.
Leaves: Made up of five or more slightly toothed and slightly lobed leaflets.
Angelica hendersonii

Cow Parsnip

Damp slopes along bluff trails; common. Gray Whale Cove Trail.
Three to six feet tall; stout stems.
Flowers: White, tiny, star-like with sickly sweet smell; clustered in flat, six-to-ten inch umbrellas. Open from huge green pods. March–May.
Leaves: Made up of three huge maple-like leaflets; one to two feet across.
Note: Look at the leaves to tell Henderson's Angelica from Cow Parsnip. Angelica leaves are made up of five or more leaflets. Cow Parsnip leaflets look like huge maple leaves.
Heracleum lanatum

White Flowers

Poison Hemlock
All trails; common.
Two to eight feet tall; purple splotches on stems.
Flowers: White, tiny; in dense umbrella-like
clusters. May–September.
Leaves: Fernlike.
Note: Poison Hemlock is deadly poisonous.
Conium maculatum

Tiny Flowers in Coils

Stinging Phacelia
Damp slopes along trails; common. Gray Whale
Cove Trail.
One to three feet tall; stinging hairs on stems.
Flowers: White, tiny; in one-to-two-inch-long
caterpillar-like coils. April–June.
Leaves: Maple-shaped, coarse with stinging hairs.
Phacelia malvifolia

Sprawling Vines

Wild Cucumber / California Manroot
All trails; common.
Fifteen to twenty feet long; mounding,
sprawling vine with coiling tendrils.
Flowers: White, five (sometimes six) petals, tiny;
male flowers in clusters along stems, female
flowers single. March–June.
Fruit: Spiny green capsules two inches in
diameter with four large seeds. May–October.
Leaves: Glossy green, slightly lobed with large
"U" at base.
Marah fabaceus

Western Morning Glory
All trails; common.
Mounding, sprawling vine.
Flowers: White, tinged with purple; funnel-
shaped. April–July.
Leaves: Arrow-shaped.
Calystegia occidentalis

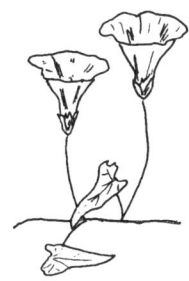

White Flowers

Fragrant Leaves

Yerba Buena
All trails; common.
Low growing and trailing, six inches to two feet long; square stems.
Flowers: White to lavender, tubular with two lips; grow where leaves join stems. May–August.
Leaves: Light-green, oval, small, fragrant; in pairs.
Satureja douglasii

Yarrow
All trails; common.
One to three feet tall; soft white hairs on stems.
Flowers: White, tiny; in dense flat-top clusters. April–October.
Leaves: Feathery and soft, dark green, fragrant.
Achillea millefolium

Mugwort
All trails; common.
One to five feet tall; stout erect stem.
Flowers: Whitish-green to whitish-yellow, tiny; in tight clusters along stems. July–August.
Leaves: Dark green above, gray-green below, very strong sage smell; lower leaves shaped like goosefeet.
Artemisia douglasiana

Pitcher Sage
Dry trails; common. Montara Mountain Trail.
Three to four feet tall; square stems.
Flowers: White to whitish-purple, tubular with large mouths, one inch long. April–June.
Leaves: Triangular, toothed, coarse-looking with an unpleasant smell.
Lepechinia calycina

White Flowers

Shrubs

Coyote Bush / Coyote Brush
All trails; common.
Three to five feet tall. Evergreen.
Flowers: White fluffy female and yellowish male on separate shrubs, small. October–December.
Seeds: Fluffy and windblown.
Leaves: Coarsely toothed, one-half to one inch long; tend to crown upper branches.
Note: Dwarf Coyote Bush (*Baccharis pilularis* var *pilularis*) grows in ground-hugging mats along Gray Whale Cove Trail.
Baccharis pilularis var *consanguinea*

Coast Sagebrush
Bluff trails; common. Gray Whale Cove Trail.
Two to four feet tall. Evergreen.
Flowers: Whitish-yellow and small; in dense clusters along ends of stems. August–October.
Leaves: Silvery-gray, finely divided and thread-like with classic sage fragrance.
Artemisia californica

Coffee Berry
All trails; common.
Four to six feet tall, compact shrub with red-purple stems. Evergreen.
Flowers: Greenish-white bells, tiny; in clusters at tips of branches. May–July.
Fruit: Green, ripening to orange, red and then black balls; in clusters. August–October.
Leaves: Dark green (often with red tips), leathery, two to four inches long; edges curl under to conserve moisture during dry summers.
Rhamnus californica

White Flowers

Thimbleberry
All trails; common. Hazelnut Trail.
Two to six feet tall; erect and softly haired stems; in dense thickets. Deciduous.
Flowers: White, five petals, one to two inches across. March–May.
Fruit: Dull-red, soft, domed berries. June–July.
Leaves: Soft, fuzzy, maple-like, five inches across.
Rubus parviflorus

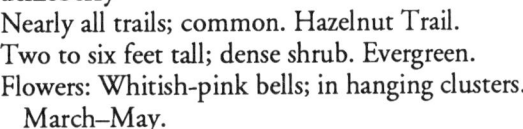

Snowberry
Nearly all trails; common.
Two to four feet tall; spreading branches. Deciduous.
Flowers: Whitish-pink to pink bells, tiny; in hanging clusters. May–June.
Fruit: White spongy balls; July–August.
Leaves: Oval with slightly wavy edges; in pairs.
Symphoricarpos albus

Huckleberry
Nearly all trails; common. Hazelnut Trail.
Two to six feet tall; dense shrub. Evergreen.
Flowers: Whitish-pink bells; in hanging clusters. March–May.
Fruit: Dark blue berries with white bloom; in tight clusters. July–September.
Leaves: Dark green with red-bronze new growth, leathery, slightly toothed, one inch long.
Vaccinium ovatum

Manzanita

Dry inland trails above 500 feet.
Four to ten feet tall; branches upright and twisted; red bark shreds easily. Evergreen.
Flowers: White, waxy dangling urns, small; in dense clusters at ends of branches. January–March.
Fruit: Reddish-green 'little apples'; in clusters. April–June.
Leaves: Slightly toothed, leathery, two-to-four inches long; in tight, upright overlapping bunches at ends of branches.
Note: Montara Manzanita *(Arctostaphylos montaraensis)* grows only on Montara Mountain. It has no burl at the base of the trunk.

Arctostaphylos sp

Cream Bush / Ocean Spray

All trails; common.
Two to fifteen feet tall; upright branches with shredding bark; tender reddish-brown new growth. Deciduous.
Flowers: Creamy white (often pale salmon pink), fade to brown and linger through the winter, tiny, fragrant; in dense showy clusters at tips of branches. April–July.
Leaves: Triangular and toothed except near base, one to three inches long; arranged alternately.

Holodiscus discolor

Yellow Flowers

4 petals

California Poppy
  Grassy trails.
  One-half to two feet tall.
  Flower: Deep orange to pale yellow, four shiny broad petals which close up on foggy days and when sun sets. March–October.
  Leaves: Silver green to dark green, finely divided.
  Note: California Poppy is the state flower.
  Eschscholzia californica

Coast Sun Cup
  Grassy trails. Gray Whale Cove Trail.
  Two inches tall.
  Flower: Bright yellow with light yellow centers, four petals. April–June.
  Leaves: Bright green; in prostrate ring.
  Camissonia ovata

Field Mustard
  Grassy trails; common. Weiler Ranch Road.
  One to four feet tall.
  Flowers: Bright yellow, four petals; in clusters on tops of stems. February–November.
  Seeds: In long narrow pods.
  Leaves: Deeply lobed lower leaves and arrow-shaped upper leaves.
  Brassica campestris

Yellow Flowers

Common Wallflower
Rocky slopes; upper North Peak Access Road. One to two feet tall.
Flowers: Yellow, four petals, one-half inch across; in dome-like clusters at tops of stems. March–May.
Leaves: Narrow and toothed.
Note: Franciscan Wallflower (*Erysimum franciscanum*), also grows on Montara Mountain. It has cream to greenish-yellow flowers. March–May.
Erysimum capitatum

Many Petals

Gum Plant
Bluff trails; common. Gray Whale Cove Trail. Four to six inches tall; in low mounds.
Flowers: Yellow with many petals, up to two inches across; sticky white gum in saucer-like flower buds. May–October.
Leaves: Oval and slightly toothed.
Grindelia stricta ssp *venulosa*

California Buttercup
Grassy trails; common. Gray Whale Cove Trail. One-half to one foot tall.
Flowers: Glistening yellow, many petals. April–June.
Leaves: Deeply cut and maple-like.
Ranunculus californicus

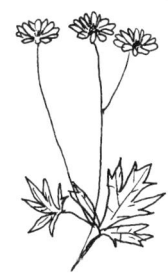

Woolly Sunflower / Oregon Sunshine
Dry trails; common. Montara Mountain Trail. Two to three feet tall; bushy.
Flowers: Bright yellow, tips turn pale yellow with age, many petals; purplish buds; in loose clusters at tops of stems. May–July.
Leaves: Dark green above and woolly below, deeply cut, fragrant.
Eriophyllum lanatum

Yellow Flowers

Rosilla
All trails.
Two to five feet tall.
Flowers: Tiny yellow petals below large brown dome-like flower centers. May–July.
Leaves: Long and narrow; form wings along stems.
Helenium puberulum

Coast Madia
All trails; common.
Two to four feet tall; stout sticky nodding stems.
Flowers: Yellow with many finely notched petals, sticky and tiny; in tight clusters at tops of stems. July–September.
Leaves: Dark green, narrow and very sticky.
Madia sativa

Sow Thistle
All trails; common.
One to four feet tall; stout red stems.
Flowers: Yellow, dandelion-like; in loose clusters at tops of stems. April–July.
Leaves: Prickly with red veins.
Sonchus oleraceus

Tiny Flowers along Stems

Beach Sagewort
Bluff trails. Gray Whale Cove Trail.
One to two feet tall.
Flowers: Yellow, tiny; in dense clusters along stems. June–October.
Leaves: Gray-green, velvety; no sage fragrance.
Artemisia pycnocephala

Yellow Flowers

Goldenrod
Nearly all trails.
Two to three feet tall.
Flowers: Yellow and tiny; in dense diamond-shaped clusters on small branches along stems. July–August.
Leaves: Long, narrow and toothed.
Solidago canadensis ssp *elongata*

Tiny Flowers in Umbrellas

Footsteps of Spring
All trails; common.
Three to eight inches tall; in prostrate mats.
Flowers: Yellow and tiny; in umbrellas at tops of short stems. February–May.
Leaves: Yellow-green, spiny, maple-like; in flat rosettes.
Sanicula arctopoides

Pacific Sanicle / Pacific Snake Root
All trails; common.
One to three feet tall; purplish rigid stems.
Flowers: Yellowish-brown, tiny; in clustered umbrellas at tops of branching stems. March–May.
Leaves: Maple-like, toothed, three inches across; near base of stem.
Sanicula crassicaulis

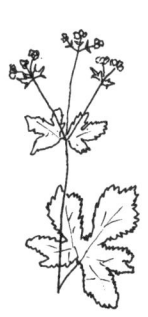

Lizard Tail
All trails; common. Gray Whale Cove Trail.
One to five feet tall; shrubby.
Flowers: Yellow, tiny; in dense umbrellas at tops of stems. May–September.
Leaves: Gray-green on top, white woolly below, deeply cut, very fragrant.
Eriophyllum staechadifolium

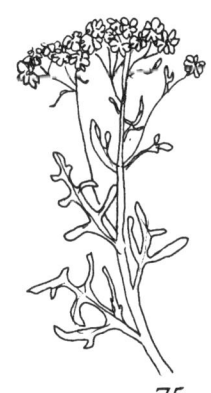

Yellow Flowers

Pea-like Flowers

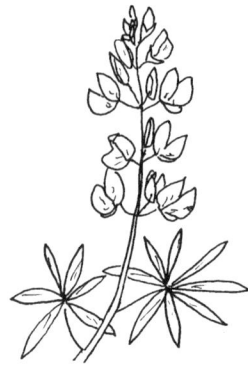

Bush Lupine / Tree Lupine
All trails; common.
Three to five feet tall. Evergreen.
Flowers: Yellow, pea-like, very fragrant; in whorls along tall stems. April–July.
Seeds: In pods.
Leaves: Dark green, five or more leaflets radiating out from centers.
Lupinus arboreus

Bird's Foot Lotus
Nearly all trails; common.
One-half to one foot tall; low spreading colonies.
Flowers: Yellow turning to red, pea-like; in clusters at tops of stems. June–August.
Leaves: Made up of three leaflets with two leaf-like structures at stems.
Lotus corniculatus

Tubular Flowers

Sticky Monkey Flower
All trails; common. Gray Whale Cove Trail.
One to four feet tall; shrubby.
Flowers: Orange and funnel-shaped with open faces, one inch long. April–October.
Leaves: Dark green and glossy, narrow, sticky; in pairs.
Note: Sticky Monkey Flowers turn the slopes of Montara Mountain golden during the summer.
Diplacus aurantiacus

Yellow Flowers

Nodding Flowers

Meadow Rue
Damp, shady trails. Old Trout Farm Trail.
Two to three feet tall.
Flowers: Light greenish-yellow with dangling thread-like flower parts; in loose clusters at tops of stems. March–May.
Leaves: Light green, three lobed leaflets per leaf.
Thalictrum polycarpum

Coast Barberry / California Mahonia
Dry trails. At the Saddle Pass.
One-half to two feet tall. Evergreen.
Flowers: Yellow and tiny, six petals; in dense clusters at tops of stems. April–June.
Fruit: Blue bloom-covered berries; in clusters.
Leaves: Glossy green (sometimes red), spiny and holly-like.
Mahonia pinnata

Shrubs

Twinberry
Moist slopes.
Five to ten feet tall; upright branches. Deciduous.
Flowers: Yellow-reddish and tubular, one-half inch long, protrude from conspicuous red papery bracts; in pairs. March–April.
Fruit: Shiny black balls; in pairs on red papery bracts. June.
Leaves: Oval and fold upward; in pairs.
Note: With age, the shiny black twin balls seem to melt into the red bracts.
Lonicera involucrata

Yellow Flowers

Succulents

Bluff Lettuce
Bluff trails and rocky trail cuts; common. Gray Whale Cove Trail.
Four to twelve inches tall; green to red succulent stems.
Flowers: Yellow, upright tubes; in tight clusters at top of stems. May–September.
Leaves: Green to red, oval and pointed; in rosette at base of stems and as triangular platforms along stems.
Dudleya farinosa

Stonecrop
Rocky trail cuts. North Peak Access Road.
Two to eight inches tall; succulent red stems.
Flowers: Yellow, five petals, star-like; in branching clusters at tops of stems. May–July.
Leaves: Gray-green and powdery; in flat rosettes at base of stems and as narrow platforms along stems.
Sedum spathulifolium

Reflections

"I went down the Ocean Shore Railroad first in the spring. Flowers were matted thick over the bluffs and the hills as though a glowing Turkish rug had been spread over all. I went again in the autumn and the rich color of the blossoms was as warmly spread as before. Poppies bloom year round, maintained in perpetual youth by the even climate and the moist airs from the ocean."
—November 8, 1914. *San Francisco Chronicle*

Red Flowers

3, 4, 5 or 7 Petals

Giant Trillium / Giant Wake Robin
Shady, moist trails. Plaskon Nature Trail.
One foot tall.
Flowers: Dark red (sometimes greenish-white), three erect petals one to two inches long; single flower directly above leaves. February–March.
Leaves: Dark green with purple blotches, large and triangular; three per plant.
Trillium chloropetalum

Coast Rock Cress
Rocky slopes. Old Pedro Mountain Road at Saddle Pass.
Up to one foot tall.
Flowers: Rose-purple to pink with white centers, four petals, up to one inch across; fragrant. March–May.
Leaves: Hairy on edges; in rosette at base of stem.
Arabis blepharophylla

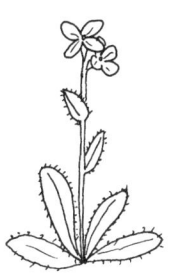

Farewell-to-Spring
Bluff trails; common. Gray Whale Cove Trail.
Up to one foot; low and sprawling.
Flowers: Pink to lavender with red centers, four ruffled petals, one to two inches across. June–July.
Leaves: Narrow and tinged with red.
Clarkia rubicunda

Red Flowers

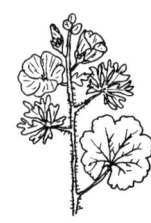

Wild Hollyhock / Checker Bloom
Dry grassy trails; common. Gray Whale Cove Trail.
One to two feet tall; sprawling, hairy stems.
Flowers: Bright pink (some with white veins), five slightly notched petals, one to two inches across; clustered along stem. March–June.
Leaves: Some rounded, some deeply cut; hairy.
Sidalcea malvaeflora

Scarlet Pimpernel
All trails; common.
Low and sprawling.
Flowers: Salmon with reddish center spot, five petals, small; close up at night. March–September.
Seeds: Small tan beads.
Leaves: Small; in pairs on stem.
Anagallis arvensis

Wild Rose
Inland trails. Hazelnut Trail.
Two to six feet tall. Thin, straight prickles on stems.
Flowers: Pink, five petals, one inch across. May–June.
Leaves: Five to seven leaflets per leaf.
Rosa gymnocarpa

Pacific Starflower
Damp, shady trails; common. Hazelnut Trail.
Two to six inches tall.
Flowers: White to deep pink, five to seven petals, starlike; one to four flowers on thin stems. March–May.
Leaves: Three to seven, of different sizes; in umbrella below flowers.
Trientalis latifolia

Red Flowers

Tiny Flowers in Balls

Sea Pink / Sea Thrift
Bluff trails; common. Gray Whale Cove Trail.
One foot tall or more; leafless stems.
Flowers: Pink, tiny; in dense, one-inch, ball-like clusters on top of one-foot stems. April–June.
Leaves: Grass-like; at base of stems.
Armeria maritima

Nodding Flowers

Fringe Cups
Shady, damp trails; common. Brooks Falls Overlook Trail.
One to three feet tall; hairy stems.
Flowers: White, red and brown; small nodding fringed cups. March–June.
Leaves: Maple-like, hairy, two to five inches wide.
Tellima grandiflora

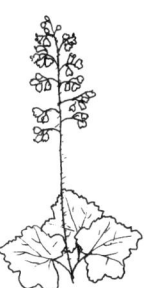

Alum Root
Damp, shady trails; common. Hazelnut Trail.
One to three feet tall; hairy stems.
Flowers: Whitish-pink, tiny; in nodding clusters along stems. April–June.
Leaves: Maple-shaped, hairy with distinctive red veins; at base of plant.
Heuchera micrantha

Salal
Dry trails. Upper Montara Mountain Trail.
Low spreading shrub.
Flowers: Pink bells, small; in loose clusters from six-inch-long red stems. May–June.
Fruit: Black balls.
Leaves: Oval with pointed tips; two to four inches long.
Gaultheria shallon

Red Flowers

Bleeding Heart
Damp, shady trails. Upper North Peak Access Road.
Two feet tall.
Flowers: Rose-purple, heart shaped, one inch long; in drooping clusters on one-to-two-foot stems. March–May.
Leaves: Fern-like and lacy, one foot long; at base of plant.
Dicentra formosa

Western Columbine
Shady, damp trails. Brooks Falls Overlook Trail.
Three or more feet tall.
Flowers: Bright red, five spurred, tubular petals which curve outward to show inner yellow flower parts; hang from stems. April–June.
Leaves: Delicate lobed leaflets; in groups of three.
Aquilegia formosa var *truncata*

Pea-like Flowers

California Milkwort
Dry, shady trails. Hazelnut Trail.
Three inches to one foot tall; many stems.
Flowers: Rose-purple, pea-like, one-half inch long; in clusters at tips of stems. March–July.
Leaves: One-half to one-and-one-half inches long, simple and smooth.
Polygala californica

Wild Sweet Pea / Everlasting Pea
Sunny, bushy trails; common.
Sprawling vine with tendrils at end of flat, winged stems.
Flowers: Bright rose-pink, pea-like, no fragrance; in clusters on erect six-to-twelve-inch flower stems. May–September.
Seeds: In pods.
Leaves: Two to four inches long; in pairs.
Lathyrus latifolius

Red Flowers

Giant Vetch
All trails; common.
Mounding vine with tendrils; smooth stems.
Flowers: Rose to red-purple, pea-like; in clusters hanging from one side of long stems. April–June.
Seeds: In pods which turn black in July.
Leaves: Up to twelve pairs of leaflets per leaf, tendril at tip.
Vicia gigantea

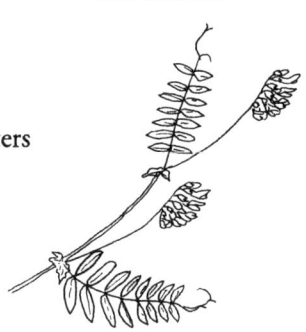

Colorful Bracts

Franciscan Paintbrush
Dry, grassy trails; common.
Two feet tall.
Flowers: Bright red bracts with bright yellow two-inch-long tube-like petals; line the stem. April–September.
Leaves: Narrow; near base of stem.
Castilleja franciscana

Coast Paintbrush
All trails; common.
One to two feet tall.
Flowers: Yellow, apricot or dull red bracts; in dense clumps at tops of stems. April–July.
Leaves: Three lobes.
Castilleja wightii

Tubular Flowers

California Bee Plant
All trails; common.
Three to six feet tall; dark red, square stems.
Flowers: Small, dark red and tubular, with longer upper petals; in clusters along stem; attract hummingbirds and bees. March–July.
Leaves: Dark green, large, triangular, coarsely toothed.
Scrophularia californica

Red Flowers

Sprawling Vine

Hairy Honeysuckle
Damp slopes. Hazelnut Trail.
Climbing, mounding, sprawling vine; reddish stems.
Flowers: Pink, trumpet shaped; in clusters at ends of stems. May–June.
Fruit: Red berries, late summer; in clusters.
Leaves: Oval and slightly hairy; in pairs; in clusters near tips of stems.
Lonicera hispidula

Thistles

Cobweb Thistle
Dry trails. Upper North Peak Access Road.
Two to four feet tall; silver-gray stems.
Flowers: Red-purple; on top of spikey ball tangled with dense cobweb-like hairs. May–June.
Leaves: Silver-gray and spiny.
Cirsium occidentale

Bull Thistle
All trails; common.
Two to six feet tall; long yellow spines on stems.
Flowers: Reddish-purple; on top of spiny ball. June–September.
Leaves: Deeply lobed with long yellow spines.
Cirsium vulgare

Shrubs

Flowering Currant
Moist slopes; common.
Three to six feet tall; upright branches with red new growth. Deciduous.
Flowers: Pink, five petals, funnel-shaped; in hanging cascades. February–April.
Fruit: Dark blue balls; in hanging clusters. July–August.
Leaves: Maple-like and soft; edges curve under.
Ribes sanguineum var *glutinosum*

Red Flowers

Coast Gooseberry
Shady damp trails. Hazelnut Trail.
Two to four feet tall; very prickly branches with long thorns. Deciduous.
Flowers: White with red at base, fuchsia-like; in hanging clusters. May–June.
Fruit: Purplish-red balls, very spiny. August.
Leaves: Hairy, maple-like, one-half to one-and-one-half inches across.
Ribes menziesii

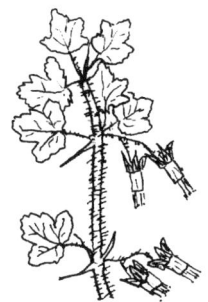

California Hazelnut
North slopes; common. Hazelnut Trail.
Five to ten feet tall. Deciduous.
Flowers: One-inch-long male catkins; September–March. Tiny reddish female flowers at joints of stems; February–April.
Fruit: Nuts; in woody shells within fuzzy husks. June–August.
Leaves: Fuzzy and toothed, roundish, one to three inches long; arranged alternately.
Corylus cornuta var *californica*

Note: Twinberry has bright red bracts which fan around twin yellow tubular flowers and twin black berries. Look for Twinberry in the Yellow Flowers section, page 77.

Attractive Dry Flower Heads

Fuller's Teasel
Grassy trails. Old Pedro Mountain Road.
Three to five feet tall. Stout stems.
Flowers: Tiny, pinkish white; in dense prickly flower heads.
Leaves: Oblong and wavy; form "wells" which fill with water where they clasp stems; in pairs.
Note: The dry, dense, prickly, brown flower heads have four long, arching spikes.
Dipsacus fullonum

Brown to Green Flowers

Fetid Adder's Tongue / Slink Pod
Damp, shady trails; common. Hazelnut Trail.
Six inches high; on short stem.
Flowers: Three down-turned greenish sepals with purple veins, three up-turned purple petals; one flower per thread-like sprawling stem; foul odor. February–March.
Leaves: Glossy green with purple spots, four to six inches long, two (sometimes three) per plant; lie flat on ground.
Scoliopus bigelovii

Mission Bells / Checker Lily
Dry trails. Hazelnut Trail.
One to three feet tall.
Flowers: Purplish-brown with green spots (sometimes greenish-yellow with purple spots), six pointed petals, bell-like, about one inch long. February–April.
Leaves: Narrow; in whorls on stem.
Fritillaria lanceolata

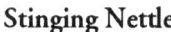

Stinging Nettle
All trails; common.
Up to six feet tall.
Flowers: Reddish-brown to greenish-white; in dangling clusters at junction of stems and leaves. April–October.
Leaves: Large, dark green, triangular, coarsely toothed; covered with poison-filled hairs.
Note: The sting from Stinging Nettles lasts for hours, if not days. Know Stinging Nettles and do not touch them.
Urtica sp

Blue Flowers

4, 5, or 6 Petals

Wild Radish
Grassy trails; common. Weiler Ranch Road.
Two to four feet tall.
Flowers: Lavender (most common), white or pink, four petals. March–August.
Seeds: In long, fat pods.
Leaves: Deeply lobed.
Raphanus sativus

Flax
Grassy trails; common. Valley View Trail.
Six inches to one foot tall.
Flowers: Pale blue, five petals, one-half inch across. April–July.
Leaves: Short and upright; cling to stems.
Linum perenne

Western Dog Violet
Grassy trails.
Two to four inches tall; in low mounds.
Flowers: Light blue to purple, five petals; on tops of long stems. March–April.
Leaves: Heart-shaped.
Viola adunca

Blue Flowers

Periwinkle
Garden escapee. Old Trout Farm Trail.
One to two feet tall; vine-like stems; spreading colonies.
Flowers: Dark blue, pinwheel-like, five petals. Nearly year around.
Leaves: Glossy, dark green, oval.
Vinca major

Hound's Tongue
Shady, moist trails; common. Brooks Falls Overlook Trail.
One to three feet tall.
Flowers: Blue with inner circle of white 'teeth,' five petals; in loose clusters at tops of stems. March–April.
Leaves: Dark green and hairy, four to six inches long; mostly at base of plant.
Cynoglossum grande

Blue Witch
All trails; common.
One to three feet tall; green stems, shrubby.
Flowers: Blue with yellow centers, wheel-like, one-half to one inch across; in loose clusters at tops of stems. February–September.
Fruit: Green balls; in hanging clusters. August–September.
Leaves: Dark green, one to two inches long.
Note: Blue Witch is poisonous.
Solanum umbelliferum

Blue-eyed Grass
Grassy trails; common.
One-half to one foot tall.
Flowers: Deep blue-purple with yellow centers, six petals with little spike on tip of each petal, one-half inch to one inch across, close up at night; at tops of stems. March–June.
Leaves: Grass-like.
Sisyrinchium bellum

Blue Flowers

Douglas Iris / Coast Iris
All trails; common. Gray Whale Cove Trail.
One to two feet tall; in colonies.
Flowers: Light blue to deep purple, three elaborate drooping sepals and three upright petals; at tops of stems. April–May.
Seeds: In upright, three-inch-long, three-sided pods.
Leaves: Grass-like and long; suffer wind and salt burn on ocean bluffs.
Iris douglasiana

Ithuriel's Spear
Grassy trails.
One-half to one foot tall; stout stem.
Flowers: Blue and funnel-like, six petals; in loose clusters at top of stem. April–June.
Leaves: Grass-like; at base of stem.
Triteleia laxa

Blue Dicks
Grassy trails, common.
One foot tall; stout stem.
Flowers: Blue, six petals, tubular; in tight clusters on top of stem. March–May.
Leaves: Grass-like; at base of stem.
Dichelostemma pulchellum

Tiny Flowers in Coils

California Coast Phacelia
Nearly all trails; common.
One to three feet tall; many stems.
Flowers: Blue, tiny; in hairy caterpillar-like coils on tops of stems. April–June.
Leaves: Made up of three leaflets with the largest in the center, dark green, fuzzy.
Phacelia californica

Blue Flowers

Many Petals

Coast Aster
Grassy trails.
One to three feet tall.
Flowers: Pale blue with yellow centers, many petals; in loose clusters. May–November.
Leaves: Long and narrow.
Aster chilensis

Seaside Daisy
Bluff trails, common. Gray Whale Cove Trail.
One-half to one foot tall; low, spreading colonies.
Flowers: Pale pink to pale lilac with yellow centers, many petals, one and one-half inches across. April–July.
Leaves: Thick and oval shaped.
Erigeron glaucus

Pea-like Flowers

Varicolored Lupine
Grassy trails; common. Gray Whale Cove Trail.
One-half to two feet tall; shrubby.
Flowers: Upper petals white, lower petals pink, lavender or blue, pea-like; in clusters at tops of stems. April–June.
Leaves: Five or more leaflets radiating from centers.
Lupinus variicolor

Fragrant Leaves

Skunkweed
All trails; common. Gray Whale Cove Trail.
Two to twelve inches tall.
Flowers: Blue, tiny, trumpet-like; clustered in spiny, pin-cushion-like balls which line stems. June–August.
Leaves: Spiny and deeply cut, strong skunk smell.
Navarretia squarrosa

Coyote Mint
All trails; common.
One to two feet tall; many upright square stems.
Flowers: Bright blue, tiny; in dense pin-cushion-like clusters on tops of stems. May–August.
Leaves: Fuzzy, dark green, oval shaped, one-half to one inch long, very fragrant; in pairs.
Monardella villosa var *franciscana*

Hedge Nettle
All trails; common.
One to two feet tall; square hairy stems.
Flowers: Light purple (sometimes white), with two lips; in whorls of six flowers along stems. March–July.
Leaves: Dark green, hairy and triangular, with strong unpleasant smell; in pairs.
Note: Hedge Nettle does not sting.
Stachys rigida var *quercetorum*

Blue Flowers

Tubular Flowers

Yerba Santa
Nearly every trail; common.
Two to five feet tall; bushy.
Flowers: Light purple, tubular, one-half inch long; in clusters at tops of stems. April–June.
Leaves: Narrow, leathery, toothed, four to six inches long; often covered with black sooty fungus.
Eriodictyon californicum

California Coast Delphinium
Damp slopes; common.
Two to five feet tall; stout red stems.
Flowers: Pale bluish-purple, one-half to one inch long with short stubby spurs; in long clusters on tops of stems. May–June.
Leaves: Deeply cut and large.
Delphinium californicum

Shrubs

California Lilac / Coast Blue Blossom
Nearly all trails; common. Hazelnut Trail.
Up to fifteen feet tall. Evergreen.
Flowers: Pale blue to bright blue, very fragrant, tiny; in dense two-to-three-inch-long clusters. March–June.
Fruit: Green ripening to black; in tight grape-like clusters. August.
Leaves: Glossy, dark green, one-half to two inches long, with three long veins meeting at base.
Ceanothus thyrsiflorus

Trees

Creek Dogwood / Red Dogwood
Creekside trails. Plaskon Nature Trail.
Up to fifteen feet tall. Red branches. Deciduous.
Flowers: White and tiny, four petals; in dense round-topped clusters two inches across. April–May.
Fruit: White balls; in umbrella-like clusters. Fall.
Leaves: Oval-shaped with pointed tips, two to four inches long.
Cornus californica

Red Elderberry
Moist slopes. Hazelnut Trail.
Up to twenty feet tall. Deciduous.
Flowers: White, tiny; in dome-like upright clusters. April–May.
Fruit: Tiny red balls; in upright clusters. May–June.
Leaves: Five to seven toothed leaflets per leaf.
Note: Red Elderberry blooms earlier than Blue Elderberry and has larger leaflets.
Sambucus callicarpa

Blue Elderberry
Moist slopes. Hazelnut Trail.
Up to twenty feet tall. Deciduous.
Flowers: White, tiny, in dense, flat-topped clusters. May–June.
Fruit: Tiny blue balls; in flat-topped clusters. July–August.
Leaves: Five to seven toothed leaflets per leaf.
Sambucus mexicana

Trees

Toyon
Nearly all trails; common. Hazelnut Trail.
Ten feet tall or more; many branches. Evergreen.
Flowers: White and small, in dense upright clusters. June–September.
Fruit: Small bright red balls; in clusters. November–December.
Leaves: Dark green, leathery, coarsely toothed, four inches long.
Note: Toyon is the state shrub.
Heteromeles arbutifolia

California Wax Myrtle
Damp slopes; Old Pedro Mountain Road.
Six to ten feet tall; many limber gray branches. Evergreen.
Flowers: Brownish-green and papery; at base of leaves along branches. April–June.
Fruit: Purplish wax-coated berries at base of leaves. September–October.
Leaves: Narrow, slightly toothed, four inches long.
Myrica californica

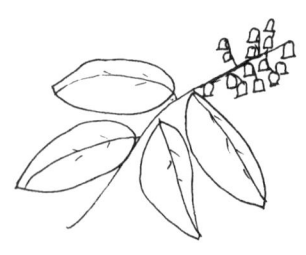

Madrone
Dry trails at higher elevations. Hazelnut Trail.
Twenty feet tall or more. Evergreen.
Flowers: White, waxy bells; in dense clusters. April.
Fruit: Orange-red berries; in hanging clusters. Summer.
Bark: Red and shredding, on smooth red wood.
Leaves: Shiny green, four to six inches long.
Arbutus menziesii

Trees

Golden Chinquapin
Dry trails at higher elevations; common. Montara Mountain Trail.
Fifteen to twenty feet tall (two to four feet tall on wind-swept slopes). Grows in groves. Evergreen.
Flowers: Creamy white, small; in showy spikes. Late summer.
Fruit: Nuts clustered in very spiny green, ripening to brown, burrs. Fall–Winter.
Leaves: Dark green above, powdery mustard-yellow below, narrow and leathery, three to six inches long; leaf tips curve under.
Castanopsis chrysophylla

Coast Silktassel
Dry trails at higher elevations. Hazelnut Trail.
Up to fifteen feet tall. Evergreen.
Flowers: Male and female catkins on separate plants; male catkins in long slender chains of "bells." January–February.
Fruit: Purple; in dangling grape-like clusters. June–September.
Leaves: Dark green above, gray below, leathery with wavy edges.
Garrya elliptica

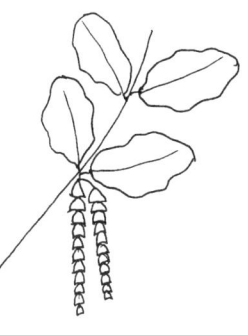

Willows
Creek trails; common. Old Trout Farm Trail.
Sizes range from shrub to tree. Grow in dense stands. Deciduous.
Flowers: Male catkins and female catkins (pussy willows) on separate plants. Catkins appear before leaves. January–February.
Seeds: Tiny; in fluffy wind-blown cotton.
Leaves: Narrow, three to five inches long.
Salix sp

Trees

Red Alder
Creekside trails. Weiler Ranch Road.
Up to forty feet tall. Deciduous.
Bark: Gray-white and patchy looking.
Flowers: Drooping male catkins. February–March.
Fruit: Green, ripening to brown, woody, cone-like female catkins; in clusters. Summer–Fall.
Leaves: Dark green, coarsely toothed, four inches long; edges tightly roll under for about one-sixteenth of an inch.
Alnus rubra

Coast Live Oak
Plaskon Nature Trail
Up to forty feet tall; broad, rounded crown. Evergreen.
Bark: Gray-green and smooth.
Fruit: Acorns in fringed caps, slender and pointed, with vertical lines on surface. Fall.
Leaves: Shiny green above, fuzzy below, sharply toothed and holly-like; edges tend to curl under.
Quercus agrifolia

Blue Gum Eucalyptus
Trails through old ranches. Brooks Falls Overlook Trail.
Fifty feet tall or more. Evergreen.
Flowers: Creamy white to yellowish, fuzzy. Winter–Spring.
Fruit: Blue-gray seed capsules, warty and ribbed, one inch across. Summer–Fall.
Leaves: Dark green, sickle-shaped, very fragrant, five to ten inches long.
Note: Blue Gum Eucalyptus trees are not native to California, but to Australia. In the late 1800s, American ranchers planted Blue Gums along San Pedro Creek and Martini Creek. Their offspring have colonized many slopes of Montara Mountain.
Eucalyptus globulus

Trees

Monterey Pine
Trails near old ranch houses and along old roads.
Fifty feet tall or more. Evergreen.
Needles: Three to seven inches long; in threes.
Cones: Lopsided and closed; in clusters which cling to trees for many years. Cones open to release seeds on very hot days and in fires.
Note: Monterey Pines are not native to Montara Mountain, but were planted by ranchers in the mid-to-late 1800s.
Pinus radiata

Monterey Cypress
Trails near old ranch houses and along old roads.
Thirty feet tall or more. Evergreen.
Cones: Round, one inch across, with "plates" that open to release seeds.
Leaves: Overlaping scales, small, very dark green; on cord-like twigs.
Note: Monterey Cypresses are not native to Montara Mountain, but were planted by ranchers in the mid-to-late 1800s.
Cupressus macrocarpa

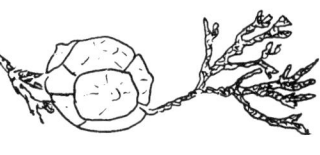

Trees

Douglas Fir
Brooks Falls Overlook Trail
Seventy feet tall or more. Evergreen.
Needles: Dark green and soft, one inch long; radiate in all directions around twigs.
Cones: Oval and narrow, two to four inches long; obvious three "mouse tails" stick out from scales; hang from branches.
Bark: Dark gray.
Note: Although native to the Bay Area, the Douglas Firs in San Pedro Valley County Park most likely were planted by early residents.
Pseudotsuga menziesii

Redwood
Brooks Falls Overlook Trail
Two hundred feet tall or more. Evergreen.
Leaves: Dark green and needle-like; grow flat from sides of twigs.
Cones: Three-quarter inch across; hang from branch tips.
Bark: Thick and shaggy, red-brown with deep furrows.
Note: A Redwood tree easily sprouts saplings from the burl at its base. Most likely early settlers planted the Redwoods in San Pedro Valley County Park.
Sequoia sempervirens

Ferns

Note: A frond is the leaf of a fern.
The pinnae are the leaflets of a frond.
Sori contain spores, the minute agents of fern reproduction.
Sori are on the underside of the pinnae.

Western Sword Fern, Coastal Wood Fern and Bracken are the most commonly seen ferns on Montara Mountain.

Western Sword Fern
   Nearly all trails; common.
   Fronds: Two to four feet long; in dense clumps.
   Pinnae: Tips slightly toothed; small "sword hilt" at base where attaches to stems.
   Sori: In rows along veins on undersides of pinnae.
   Polystichum munitum

Coastal Wood Fern
   Shady trails; common. Lower Montara Mountain Trail.
   Fronds: One to two feet long; in open, graceful clumps; look ruffled.
   Pinnae: Fringed tips and sides.
   Sori: In two rows on undersides of pinnae.
   Dryopteris arguta

Bracken Fern / Brake
   Nearly all trails; common.
   Fronds: Two to four feet long, broad triangles; on single stems (non-clumping).
   Pinnae: Leathery.
   Sori: In dense rows around edges of undersides of pinnae.
   Pteridium aquilinum var *pubescens*

Ferns

Golden Back Fern
Damp, shady trail cuts. Brooks Falls Overlook Trail.
Fronds: Two to five inches long. Bright black stems.
Pinnae: Dark green above and powdery yellow below.
Sori: Dark black, densely outline the veins of undersides of pinnae.
Pityrogramma triangularis

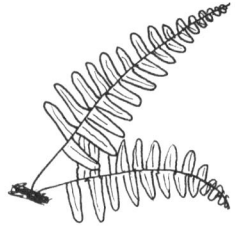

California Polypody
Bluff trails; common. Gray Whale Cove Trail.
Fronds: One foot long; in clusters.
Pinnae: Round tips.
Sori: In rows along edges of undersides of pinnae.
Polypodium californicum

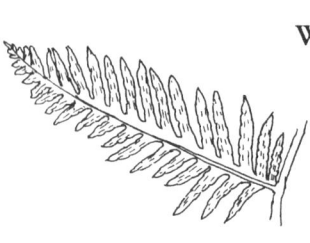

Western Chain Fern
Creek banks. Plaskon Nature Trail.
Fronds: Six feet long; radiate outward from central clumps.
Pinnae: Scalloped and slightly toothed; obvious "chain" or "stitch" along veins.
Sori: In chains along veins on undersides of pinnae.
Woodwardia fimbriata

Lady Fern
Creek banks. Plaskon Nature Trail.
Fronds: Four feet long; radiating from central clumps.
Pinnae: Light green and delicate looking.
Sori: Oval or horseshoe-shaped; along veins on undersides of pinnae.
Athyrium filix-femina

Grasses

Note: Three noticable non-native grasses grow on Montara Mountain: Pampas Grass, Rattlesnake Grass and Wild Oats.

Pampas Grass
Old road and trail cuts.
Six to seven feet tall and four to five feet wide.
Flowers: Showy golden plumes; along ends of stems. Fall.
Leaves: Sharply toothed and dangerous.
Seeds: Fluffy and windblown.
Note: Pampas Grass is an aggressive, invasive alien which crowds out native Coastal Scrub vegetation.
Cortaderia jubata

Rattlesnake Grass / Big Quaking Grass
Old grazing grounds; common. Valley View Trail.
One-half to one foot tall.
Drooping pannicles shaped like rattlesnake tails; rattle in the wind.
Note: Delicate Little Quaking Grass (*Briza Minor*) lines Hazelnut Trail.
Briza maxima

Wild Oats
Old grazing grounds; common.
One to two feet tall.
Nodding pannicles with long "tails."
Note: Wild Oats came with the Spanish and their longhorn cattle in the 1790s.
Avena fatua

Reflections

"Spring has camped on the coastside hills and spread her emerald mantle abroad. The golden California poppies—the *capra de oro* of the Padres—make patches of flame in the sunshine. Trillium and King Solomon's seal lift their creamy white beauty in sedgy places, and pink clusters of wild current bush fling forth their beauty and fragrance where canyons slip down from the mountain side. And wonderful purple iris peeps at you from unexpected places. And the meadowlark sings to the blue sky the glory to God. Go ye to the hills and learn."

—George E. Dunn. March 5, 1920. *Coast Side Comet*

—6—

Wildlife on Montara Mountain

All animals on Montara Mountain are wild and they deserve respect. Along Weiler Ranch Road in San Pedro Valley County Park, you may feel as if you were walking through an open air zoo—Bobcats crouch in the meadows, Mule Deer graze the grasses, Brush Rabbits nibble along the trailside, California Quail cluck as you pass and Merriam Chipmunks frolic around the far bench. Please don't approach or feed them. They do quite well for themselves along the lush valley of the Middle Fork of San Pedro Creek.

The best places to watch for birds in McNee Ranch State Park are along Martini Creek and along Gray Whale Cove Trail, especially in the lush dells. In San Pedro Valley County Park, look for birds in the picnic areas and along the two forks of San Pedro Creek.

Brush Rabbit

Mammals

Gray Fox: Most likely, you will see signs of Gray Fox, but not a Gray Fox itself. On all trails, look for small mounds of gray, furry scat, the sign that a Gray Fox has loped along ahead of you. The furry scat indicates a diet laden with furry rodents, although Gray Foxes also eat Coffee Berries, Manzanita berries and Toyon berries. They are excellent tree climbers. If you come upon a disturbed Wood Rat nest, chances are a Gray Fox dined on the inhabitant.

A Gray Fox stands about two feet tall, has short legs, brownish red sides and a dark stripe continuing down its back and bushy tail. It easily blends into the light and shadow of Coastal Scrub.

Coyote: Around sunset, Coyotes sometimes send out crying yips across Montara Mountain—but you probably will never see them. Mangy-looking, grayish-brown Coyotes are about the size of German shepherds.

Coyotes eat small mammals.

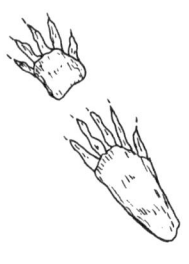
Raccoon track

Raccoon: After dusk, once the parks on Montara Mountain are closed, Raccoons come out to forage in the picnic areas and along the creeks. In the morning, you might see their hand-like tracks in damp soil. Raccoons are easily recognized by their bandit eye masks and ringed tails.

Raccoons eat almost anything, from lizards to birds' eggs to berries. If you see half-dollar size balls of scat festooned with Coffee Berry seeds along the trail, you know a raccoon has passed by.

Stripped Skunk: Skunks are more often smelled than seen. If you do see one, it will be about the size of a large house cat and have a very bushy black tail with two large white stripes running along its back. Skunks spray tormentors only as a final "stay-away" warning.

Skunks live near creeks and eat insects and small rodents.

Wildlife on Montara Mountain

Bobcat: On Weiler Ranch Road, you may see Bobcats sitting in the meadows, slowing turning their heads from left to right as they scan for small mammals to ambush. Hikers don't seem to alarm them, although Bobcats can alarm hikers who see them pounce on Merriam Chipmunks and Brush Rabbits.

Bobcats have mottled-colored coats, tufted ears and short, bobbed tails, and are the size of a very large, muscular house cat. They are strictly carnivores.

Mountain Lion: Yes, Mountain Lions—and their tracks—have been seen on Montara Mountain, but not frequently. Some people call them Cougars. They are more than twice the size of Bobcats, have long tails and are tawny colored.

Mountain Lions eat deer.

Merriam Chipmunk: Along Hazelnut Trail in San Pedro Valley County Park, you will most certainly be scolded by Merriam Chipmunks hiding in the Coyote Bush. At first you may think the high-pitched chattering is a bird, but look more closely. The chipmunk gives its hiding place away each time it chirps by nervously throwing its head back and sharply twitching its tail. You can also see these dark brown, lightly striped chipmunks near the last bench on Weiler Ranch Road.

Merriam Chipmunks eat seeds, nuts and berries.

Pocket Gopher: Look for freshly dug gopher mounds in the meadows in San Pedro Valley County Park. Some folks call Gophers "Natures' plows." Other folks have less kind words. A Gopher has four sharp yellow incisor teeth which together can grow up to 46 inches a year. But the teeth are kept pared down to a manageable size by constant tunnel digging and plant harvesting.

Gophers are vegetarians and eat the roots, leaves and flowers of meadow plants. Owls, hawks, coyotes and foxes eat gophers.

Montara Mountain

Dusky-footed Wood Rat or Pack Rat: You will probably never see a Wood Rat, but you will certainly see plenty of Wood Rat nests along nearly every trail on Montara Mountain. These nocturnal animals spend hours gathering sticks to pile together to make their houses, some of which are over four feet tall. People who have dismantle nests find them a complex net of interwoven sticks, hallways, rooms and tenants, including lizards, snakes and insects. Yes, Wood Rats do collect odd bits and pieces that humans leave about. Gray Foxes are their main enemy.

Wood Rats are vegetarians and eat acorns, seeds, fruit and plants.

Brush Rabbit: A Brush Rabbit never ventures more than a few feet from sheltering thickets in its quest for plants to nibble. Its bright eyes, tiny white tail, short ears and brown fur attract the attention of hikers—and of predators.

Opossum: Nocturnal Opossums live near creeks on Montara Mountain. These marsupials, imported from the East Coast, thrive on Coastal Scrub vegetation, birds' eggs, insects and small mammals.

Mule Deer / Black-tailed Deer: Mule Deer, twitching their short, dark tails, browse the Coastal Scrub of Montara Mountain and follow the trails cut by man. After a heavy fog or rain, the damp soil of most trails shows Mule Deer tracks. In the summer, look for nibbled down stalks of California Bee Plant along the trails. Mule Deer also enjoy Huckleberries, Coffee Berries, Blackberries and Coyote Bush. The bucks show magnificent antlers in the fall. In the spring, you may see fawns along Weiler Ranch Road.

Mule Deer track

Lizards

Western Fence Lizard: Nine times out of ten, a rustling in the dry leaves along the trail's edge means either a Western Fence Lizard or an Alligator Lizard is near. Both are between five and eight inches long. Western Fence Lizards have blue bellies and bluish-white markings on their backs The males do "push-ups" to scare off challengers.

Western Fence Lizards are not aggressive. They eat insects and spiders.

Alligator Lizard: An alligator snout, a fold of skin running between front and back legs along both sides of its body, and light brown scales identify an Alligator Lizard. These aggressive lizards feed on insects and spiders.

Molluscs

Banana Slug: Mustard-yellow Banana Slugs, sometimes called Nature's Little Composters, slide along the moist forest floor under dripping Blue Gum Eucalyptus trees. These harmless, shell-less molluscs, sometimes reaching seven inches long, slowly process plant debris. Quite often you will find them slowly inching across the trail ahead.

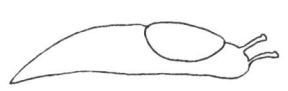

Birds

Note: Use these sketches for a quick guide to some of the common year-round birds found on Montara Mountain.

Turkey Vulture: Turkey Vultures ride the thermals across Montara Mountain looking for dead animals. Tilting from side to side, they hold their wings in a slight V. Use binoculars to see their featherless red heads. The upper half of their wings are black, the lower half dark gray.
Length 25 inches; wingspan 72 inches.

Red-tailed Hawk: Look for soaring Red-tailed Hawks year-round. The high screeching cry, broad wings spanning four feet, dark belly band and red upper tail feathers identify this handsome bird. Red-tails eat rodents.
Length 18 inches; wingspan 48 inches.

American Kestrel: Fall and winter are the best times to spot American Kestrels perching on tree tops. Sometimes they drop on insects from their perches, other times they hover over meadows before dropping. Colorful Male Kestrels have blue-gray wings, red-brown backs and crowns, and dark black stripes down white necks. The larger females have red-brown wings, backs and crowns and paler stripes on white necks. Their *killy, killy* cry is unmistakable.
Length 9 inches; wingspan 21 inches.

Wildlife on Montara Mountain

Raven: More and more Ravens now soar over Montara Mountain. Ravens are rarely alone; sometimes you will see as many as six or more riding the thermals, often in what seems to be play. Ravens are deep black and have heavy bills. In flight note their wedge-shaped tails. Their call is a harsh *wroock*. Ravens eat nearly everything, including dead animals.
Length 21 inches.

California Quail: Coveys of California Quail feed on seeds, grasses and berries along Weiler Ranch Road. Occasionally you will hear an unmistakable *ja-JA-ja* call, but mostly listen for full-throated clucking. The males, with curved black head plumes, black bibs ringed with white, and bluish chests, often stand guard on top of a Coyote Bush. Females have smaller head plumes. Both have white flecked bellies. Quail are fast runners, but ponderous fliers. California Quail is the state bird.
Length 10 inches.

Mourning Dove: Aptly named, the Mourning Dove has a very sad, plaintive *whoo-oo* call. Look for flocks feeding on the ground near creeks. These small-headed, gray, sculptured-looking birds have long pointed tails. When they take flight, their wings whistle.
Length 11 inches.

Anna's Hummingbird: To spot a male Anna's Hummingbird on its perch, listen for its song, a sound like a finger scratching across a chalkboard. Then look for a brilliant flash of iridescent red as it turns its head and neck back and forth in the sunlight. Females have white necks tinged with red and the same green body as males. Anna's Hummingbirds use their long tongues to gather insects and nectar.
Length 4 inches.

Montara Mountain

Red-shafted Flicker: Red-shafted Flickers fly across the Coastal Scrub in a series of undulating waves, folding their wings tight to their bodies on the down side of the wave and flapping them on the up side. Look for red underwings and tails, white rumps, black bibs and speckled chests. Their long, strong bills are useful for digging out insects in tree trunks. Flickers often give a loud sharp *flick* as they take flight.
Length 11 inches.

Black Phoebe: A solitary bird with a square, black head, black back and chest, and white belly perched on a small branch will be a Black Phoebe. Watch it flick its tail before taking off after an insect. Black Phoebes often return to the same perch over and over again. They have a plaintive call—*ti-wee, ti-wee*.
Length 6 inches.

Scrub Jay: Raucous Scrub Jays range over all of Montara Mountain. They have blue heads, tails and wings, and white chests—but no head crests. They eat almost everything. Their call—*jay, jay*—will accompany every hike you take.
Length 10 inches.

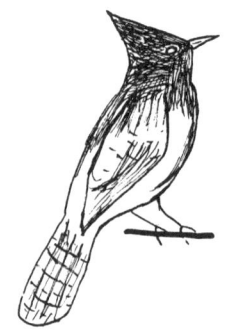

Stellar's Jay: Stellar's Jays have black head crests and brilliant blue feathers in various shades. Their call, a very raucous *jay, jay, jay*, is heard most frequently near where people—and their garbage—hang out. Stellar's Jays can successfully imitate the screech of Red-tailed Hawks and the rasp of a rusty gate.
Length 11 inches.

Wildlife on Montara Mountain

Chestnut-backed Chickadee: Chickadees are abundant along creeks on Montara Mountain. Their *chick-a-dee* calls, black caps, black throats and brown backs are distinctive, as is their acrobatic foraging in trees and shrubs.
Length 4 inches.

Bushtit: Tiny, gray Bushtits travel through the Coastal Scrub in flocks, giving out high, wheezy twitters as they dangle from twigs and leaves in their search for insects. Their tails seem too long for their little round bodies.
Length 4 inches.

Wrentit: You will most certainly hear but probably not see Wrentits on Montara Mountain. Some folks liken the call of a Wrentit to the sound of a ping-pong ball bouncing on a tabletop. Look for a dark brown bird with light eyes and a long upright tail hopping secretively from branch to branch in the Coyote Bush.

Wrentits and Coastal Scrub go together. The destruction of Coastal Scrub means the destruction of the habitat for these birds.
Length 5 inches.

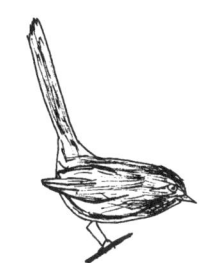

Winter Wren: This tiny, brown wren with a stubby upright tail bobs along on low-lying branches near creeks. It has a light line over its eyes and stripes on its lower belly. You will probably see a Winter Wren if you sit for a while on the bench on Plaskon Nature Trail.
Length 3 inches.

Bewick's Wren: A Bewick's Wren will vigorously scold you from deep inside a Coyote Bush if you come within its territory. Look closely to see its brown back, white belly and whitish upright tail. The long white line across its eyes is distinctive. Pronounce Bewick's as "Buick's."
Length 5 inches.

Montara Mountain

California Thrasher: Liquid musical notes of pure joy spread over the Coastal Scrub when a California Thrasher lights atop a Coyote Bush. These brown birds have long downward curved bills which they use to scratch aside dead leaves in their search for insects. If startled, they tend to run along the ground with their tails held upright.
Length 11 inches.

Robin: A rotund red chest, dark gray back, white eye ring and cheery call mean just one bird—a Robin. Look for Robins searching for insects and worms around the picnic areas in San Pedro Valley County Park.
Length 10 inches.

Starling: The color of stubby-tailed Starlings is changeable: in the summer look for glossy purplish-black plumage and yellow bills; in the winter look for glossy brownish-black plumage, white speckled chests and brown bills. Starlings have a squeaky call, but they also can imitate musical birds. Starlings forage and roost near the picnic areas in San Pedro Valley County Park.
Length 7 inches.

Rufous-sided Towhee: Colorful Rufous-sided Towhees perch on top of the Coyote Bush or rustle in the dry leaves below looking for seeds and insects. Their black heads, white bellies, reddish-brown sides, and black wings speckled with white contrast vividly with the somber greens of Coastal Scrub. Some folks hear *drink-your-tea* in their song.
Length 7 inches.

Brown Towhee: Brown Towhees are exactly that—brown (except for a faint touch of orange under their tails). These birds scratch for insects on the ground under Coastal Scrub. They are common Bay Area backyard birds, known by their *tink, tink* call.
Length 8 inches.

Oregon Junco: A black head and neck, dark brown back, pink bill and white belly make an Oregon Junco look like a monk in a cowl. These bold seed eaters are found all over Montara Mountain during the winter months.
   Length 5 inches.

House Sparrow: House Sparrows chirp noisily—no one would call them songbirds. The males have black bibs and gray crowns; the females don't. Both have streaked brown backs and unstreaked lighter chests. Look for them around the picnic areas in San Pedro Valley County Park.
   Length 5 inches.

House Finch: In the spring as you walk along the creekside trails, listen for the warbling song of House Finches. The males have red crowns, chests and rumps. Note the obvious streaked chests of the females. House Finches are seed eaters.
   Length 5 inches.

White-crowned Sparrow: White-crowned Sparrows and Coyote Bush seem made for each other. Look for these seed eaters: 1. singing joyously from the top of a Coyote Bush; 2. resting in the middle of a Coyote Bush; and 3. feeding under a Coyote Bush. Three white head-stripes make the crown; chests are gray and unstreaked; backs are brown.
   Length 6 inches.

Song Sparrow: Listen along creekside trails for the melodious song of a Song Sparrow. Note the brown chest stripes which join in a large center-of-the-chest spot. Song Sparrows have brown backs and white chests.
   Length 6 inches.

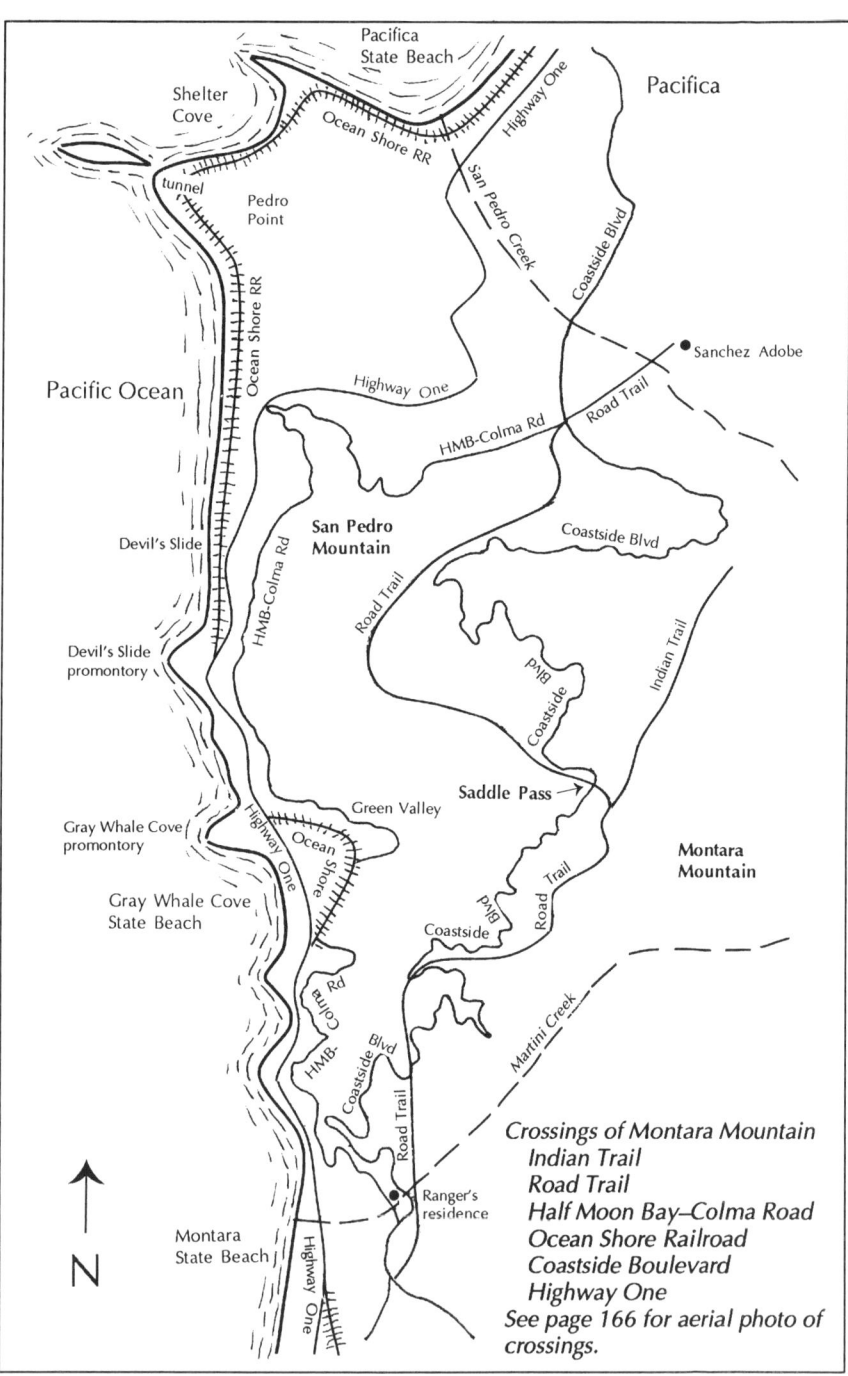

~7~

Crossings of Montara Mountain

Montara Mountain is formidable. Within a distance of two miles—from the shoreline to North Peak (1,898 feet)—sheer ocean bluffs, steep-walled canyons and narrow ridges block any easy north–south passage. Yet for thousands of years, people needed to cross the mountain. Over time, they blazed two crossings. One crossing runs inland over the Saddle Pass, which separates Montara Mountain from San Pedro Mountain. The other crossing runs along steep bluffs, where Montara Mountain and San Pedro Mountain drop abruptly into the Pacific Ocean.

• **The Saddle Pass crossing:** When you stand at the Saddle Pass in McNee Ranch State Park, you stand where Native American Costanos crossed the mountain; where northbound Spanish explorers most likely halted to get their bearings; where Spanish Mission fathers and Costano vaqueros drove cattle south to grasslands near Pillar Point; where Mexican land grant holders cantered by to reach their cattle ranches; where American ranchers paused to rest pack trains; and where motorists parked overheated Model T Fords.

• **The ocean bluff crossing:** When you drive Highway One along the ocean bluffs, you drive where passengers in Ocean Shore Railroad trains gasped at the awesome views; and where teamsters drove their creaking wagons along a road just uphill.

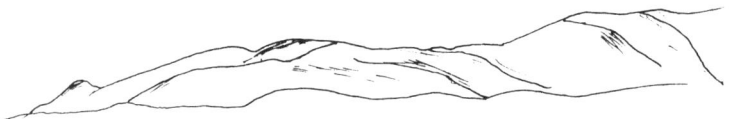

Native American Crossings (for at least 5,000 years before 1769)

Before the arrival of Europeans, Native Americans walked the ridges of Montara Mountain to exchange visits between the village of Pruristac on San Pedro Creek (near the Sanchez Adobe) and the village of Ssatumnumo on Pilarcitos Creek (in Half Moon Bay). They gathered shellfish along the rocky ocean shores, hunted rabbits, deer and birds on the slopes of Montara Mountain, picked California blackberries, huckleberries and hazelnuts in the sheltered canyons, and harvested grass seeds from the broad coastal terraces. Today, two shell middens mark Native American campsites: one on the bank of Martini Creek near Montara State Beach parking lot and the other on the bank of San Pedro Creek near the Linda Mar Recycling Center.

What the Native Americans called their trail over Montara Mountain is unknown. In 1866 American mapmakers, drawing up one of the first maps of Montara Mountain, chose to call it the "Indian Trail."

> **Traces of the Indian Trail**
> Native American trails tended to take the easiest routes over mountains. The Indian Trail over Montara Mountain most likely followed the ridge lines behind the Willow Brook Estates neighborhood in San Pedro Valley up to the Saddle Pass, and then took the high ridge above Green Valley to wind down to Martini Creek near the Ranger's residence in McNee Ranch State Park.
>
> In McNee Ranch State Park, hike North Peak Access Road uphill from Gray Whale Cove Overlook. Above you on the ridge top is a remnant of the Indian Trail, which after one-half mile bends downslope to the Saddle Pass.

Crossings of Montara Mountain

Gaspar de Portolá stands with his back to the Pacific Ocean, contemplating Sweeney Ridge. The monument is at the corner of Highway One and Crespi Drive in the Linda Mar district of Pacifica.

Spanish Crossings (1769–1821)

No one knows the exact route the Spanish explorer Gaspar de Portolá and his men took over Montara Mountain in October of 1769. What is known is that they travelled north from a campsite on Martini Creek to a campsite on San Pedro Creek—

> "on a very bad road up over a very high mountain... The high hills which forbade us a way along the sea-shore, though easily climbed on the way up, had a very hard abrupt descent on the opposite side... We stopped upon the height; here 25 heathens came up..."[1]

Note that the explorers mentioned using "a very bad road," at the crest of which they met travelling Costanos (their name for the Native Americans). Most likely, Portolá was on what came to be known as the Indian Trail, which crossed the mountain at the Saddle Pass.

For Portolá and his men, Montara Mountain was just one more obstacle on their journey north from San Diego along the

---

[1] Stanger and Brown, pp. 93-96.

Montara Mountain

Pacific shoreline. They had missed their destination of Monterey Bay. But just ahead, once across Montara Mountain and atop Sweeney Ridge on the northeast side of San Pedro Valley, they would see a far grander bay—San Francisco Bay.

Within a few years, Spanish Mission fathers marched to the tip of the San Francisco Peninsula, established Mission Dolores, and then reached south along the coast to set up an outpost ranch, named San Pedro y San Pablo, in San Pedro Valley. The well-watered, fertile valley, plus the forced labor of Costanos, provided vegetables, grain and beef to feed Mission Dolores. In the 1790s, after an epidemic killed most of the Costano laborers, the Mission fathers drove their cattle over the Saddle Pass to graze on the lush coastal terrace of the bay of Half Moon Bay.

Once established south of Montara Mountain, the Spanish blazed an easier trail east up Pilarcitos Creek (in Half Moon Bay), crossing the Santa Cruz Mountains to reach both the bayside and San Francisco. From then until the early 1900s, travellers far preferred this route (now used by Highway 92) to the steep and winding roads on Montara Mountain.

You can hike to the Discovery Site monument on top of Sweeney Ridge from both Pacifica and San Bruno. (See page 36.) The plaque on the monument reads:

> FROM THIS RIDGE
> THE
> PORTOLÁ EXPEDITION
> DISCOVERED
> SAN FRANCISCO BAY
> NOVEMBER 4, 1769

Traces of Spanish Crossings
Most likely the Spaniards followed the Indian Trail along the ridge lines over Montara Mountain. You can trace a bit of Portolá's route at the Saddle Pass in McNee Ranch State Park.

The Sanchez Adobe on Linda Mar Boulevard in Pacifica. The Adobe, a living museum, lets you experience California history from the days of the Native Americans through the notorious Prohibition years. The Adobe is open to the public. (See page 37.)

Mexican Crossings (1821–1848)

In 1821, after the revolution against Spain, California became Mexican. Longhorn cattle continued to graze the slopes of Montara Mountain but the Mission fathers were no more. In 1839 their land on the mountain became part of two land grants: Rancho San Pedro and Rancho Corral de Tierra Palomares.

In 1846 Francisco Sanchez, owner of the Rancho San Pedro land grant, built his home—the Sanchez Adobe—in San Pedro Valley on the ruins of the old Spanish outpost. With the passage of time, the adobe became a hotel, a hunting lodge, a bootleg saloon and an artichoke packing shed. San Mateo County bought the old adobe in 1947. Today, restored as Francisco Sanchez's home, it is a museum worth visiting.

Francisco Guerrero–Palomares, owner of Rancho Corral de Tierra Palomares, built an adobe on the bank of Denniston Creek north of El Granada, but he lived in San Francisco. The adobe was torn down in 1911.

Both Sanchez and Guerrero–Palomares were cattle ranchers and officials in the Mexican government.

Montara Mountain

Much of McNee Ranch State Park and most of San Pedro Valley Park lie outside the old land grants.

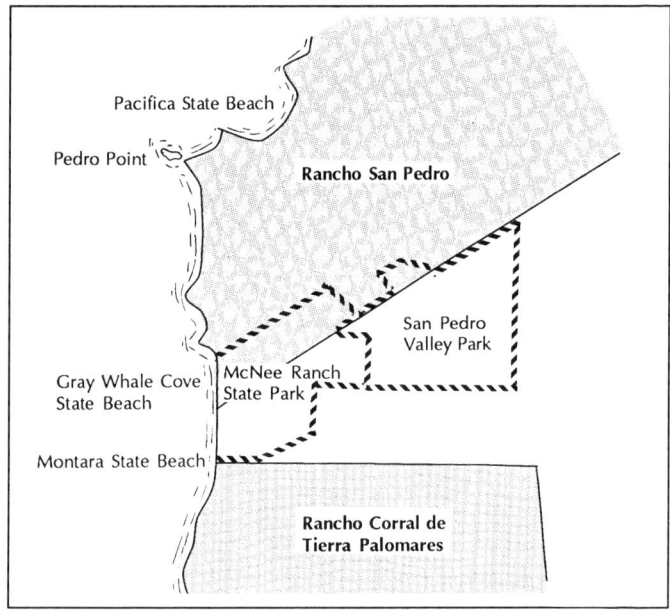

Sketch map of Mexican land grant boundaries on Montara Mountain and San Pedro Mountain.

The southern boundary of Rancho San Pedro sliced across Montara Mountain from just south of Gray Whale Cove, across Green Valley to the Saddle Pass, and through the Visitor Center at San Pedro Valley County Park.

The northern boundary of Rancho Corral de Tierra Palomares ran in a straight line due east from Montara State Beach parking lot at Martini Creek.

Today, Rancho San Pedro is the City of Pacifica. Montara, Moss Beach, Princeton and El Granada occupy part of Rancho Corral de Tierra Palomares.

> **Traces of Mexican Crossings**
> A Mexican map from 1839 calls the crossing *Camino Pedro Cuesta,* Pedro Grade Road. It most likely followed the ridges and crossed at the Saddle Pass.

Road Trail (1848–1879)

At the end of the Mexican–American War in 1848, California became part of the United States. One of the first American maps of the San Mateo County coast, the U. S. Coast Survey of 1866, showed two trails—Indian Trail and Road Trail—over Montara Mountain. Both crossed at the Saddle Pass.

Most likely, the Costanos, Spanish and Mexicans had used what became known as the Road Trail. But the Coastside ranchers, who came next, considered the Road Trail impassable. To get their grain and potatoes to San Francisco markets, they built two shipping wharfs on the bay of Half Moon Bay and sent their crops out by boat.

Here is what two travellers thought of the Road Trail—

> "That night [in June of 1856] we were only to ride to Denniston's rancho at Half Moon Bay, a distance of about twenty-five miles from the Mission [in San Francisco], in what is now the county of San Mateo. We had to traverse a rugged mountain road, bad enough in the day-time, but at night, except on the surest-footed beasts, almost impassable."
> —Edward McGowen. 1856

> "It took two hours to go over San Pedro Mountain by horse. It is doubtful if a wheeled vehicle ever went over the road."   —October 19, 1872. *San Mateo County Gazette*

> **Traces of the Road Trail**
> The Road Trail ran via the Saddle Pass between a ranch on Martini Creek and the Sanchez Adobe on San Pedro Creek.
>
> At the Saddle Pass in McNee Ranch State Park, look oceanward to note the broad trail that scars the slope of San Pedro Mountain. This trail, the legacy of the Road Trail, continues for about one-half mile before taking the ridge which dips to the Linda Mar district of Pacifica.
>
> At the Saddle Pass, walk inland a few hundred feet to note a massive granite outcrop. The Road Trail was on the ridge above. It wound down to the Saddle Pass behind the granite outcrop.
>
> The Indian Trail followed the ridge just inland from the Saddle Pass, down to Willow Brook Estates in Linda Mar.

Montara Mountain

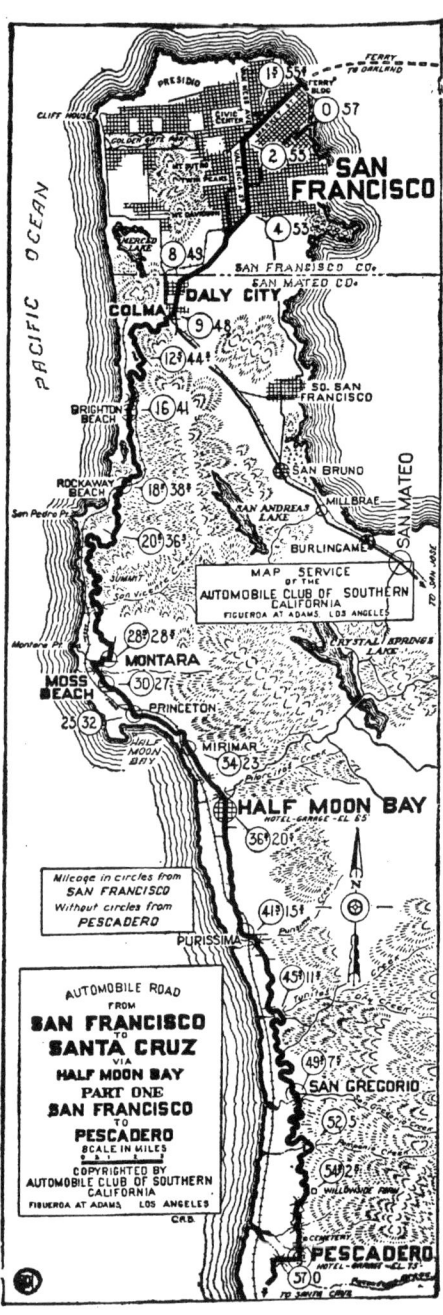

Map from the early 1910s of the Half Moon Bay–Colma Road between San Francisco and Half Moon Bay. The map didn't indicate how treacherous the road was.

[Courtesy Duncan Nanney]

Crossings of Montara Mountain

[Courtesy The Bancroft Library]
In 1914 only the stout-hearted attempted the Half Moon Bay–Colma Road. For years, the road had been so bad that farmers shipped their produce to San Francisco by boat.

Half Moon Bay–Colma Road (1879–1915)

The steep and rutted Road Trail, never a proper road, infuriated the residents of San Pedro Valley and Half Moon Bay. In the late 1870s, spurred by a barrage of angry petitions, the San Mateo County Board of Supervisors voted to abandon it—and with it the Saddle Pass crossing of Montara Mountain.

The new road—the Half Moon Bay–Colma Road—sliced cleanly along the ocean bluffs. The section between Martini Creek and Green Valley was quite straight forward: It was a relatively flat, single-lane road at about the 200-foot contour line. But the section between Green Valley and San Pedro Valley was a nightmare. The road wound deep into Green Valley before swinging back oceanward for the steep, winding ascent up the southern flank of San Pedro Mountain to the top of Devil's Slide. It then ran along the top of the bluffs before dropping down into the valley of Shamrock Ranch in the Linda Mar district of Pacifica. The steepest grade was 24%; the average grade was 18%. (A 24% grade means that for every 100 feet of road, the elevation of the road increases by 24 feet. For comparison, on Old Pedro Mountain Road in McNee Ranch State Park, no grade is greater than 7%.)

Montara Mountain

[Courtesy The Bancroft Library]

1914. The southern slope of San Pedro Mountain at the Devil's Slide promontory. You can still trace the Half Moon Bay–Colma Road as it hairpins to the top.

[Courtesy The Bancroft Library]

1914. The promontory at Devil's Slide is in the background.

Crossings of Montara Mountain

The Half Moon Bay–Colma Road opened in 1879, but within a few years residents fumed—

> "The San Pedro Road connecting Half Moon Bay to Colma is in a most deplorable and dangerous condition... The road as built and maintained to present day is an abomination and merely an apology for a road, as it was never built to grade."
> —August 2, 1897.
> Petition to the San Mateo County Board of Supervisors

In 1907 when the Ocean Shore Railroad built its roadbed along the San Pedro Mountain ocean bluffs, the Half Moon Bay–Colma Road above threatened to collapse. Ocean Shore engineers offered to move the road inland to the Saddle Pass, but the County Board of Supervisors refused.

A Trip on Horseback in 1911

> "The road [north from Half Moon Bay] came again to the shore at Montara Point, where there is a small lighthouse. A mile ahead a fine mountain came sharply to the sea, and I could trace a road graded steeply over it. I had not expected another taste of the mountains so near as I now was to San Francisco, and I rejoiced at the sight. We soon began the climb, which brought magnificent views of cliff and sea, often several hundred feet almost sheer below.
>
> "The mist lay thickly over the water at a little distance from the shore, and I had to leave to the mind's eye the view I had anticipated, of the sails or smoke of many vessels making to the Golden Gate. From the summit of the grade [above Devil's Slide] I looked out to the north upon the green valley of San Pedro and the long line of cliff shore that runs to the entrance of the great bay. Below, the fine headland of San Pedro Point stood out to the west, ending in a picturesque little island pinnacled like an iceberg; and farther to the north I could just discern the outline of the high, bold coast of Marin.
>
> "A steep descent followed by a few miles of monotonous road brought us to Laguna Salada..."
> —Smeaton Chase, 1911

Montara Mountain

[Courtesy The Bancroft Library]

1914. The Half Moon Bay–Colma Road. "There is no road running along the ocean that is more interesting, more grand and sublime than this road. It is, however, almost impossible, except for the expert, to drive on." —March, 1914. Motoring Magazine

[Courtesy The Bancroft Library]

1914. One of the worst hairpin turns on San Pedro Mountain near the top of Devil's Slide. "The grade and turns are of such a nature, having been laid out for the use of horses, that it is dangerous for the ordinary car driver." —April, 1914. Motoring Magazine

A Trip by Automobile in 1912

"Automobilists who revel in exciting journeys where the source of excitement does not depend upon speed, but upon the nature of the road and its scenic surprises, could find no trip close to San Francisco which would more meet with their approval than to duplicate the journey of The Call's Studebaker-Flanders '20' pathfinding party last Sunday, when a trip from this city down the coast to Halfmoon Bay was made.

"The route is one which is seldom visited by automobiles, and The Call's car enjoys the distinction of being the first machine to make the trip, not only this season, but the first car in many months to do so. The last car attempting to accomplish this task met with disaster in which the driver and occupants had a remarkable escape from death.

"Pedro Point stands out as the most striking feature of the scenery and its ruggedness holds the spectator while he recalls with a half shudder the treachery that lurks in the rocky jaws of the point and the fate of the many vessels that have been pounded to pieces in its hold.

"Leaving peaceful Pedro Valley, one immediately commences the ascent of the ridge just back of Point Pedro. For two miles the car winds up the side of the mountain over as treacherous a piece of road as can be found. Death stalks in front and lurks behind in every foot of the climb to the summit [top of Devil's Slide]. There are hairpin turns aplenty, but none of them baffled The Call's Studebaker-Flanders. The grade all the way to the top runs from 6 to 20 percent, and while The Call's car exhibited an abundance of power in the intermediate gear, it was necessary to drop into low gear often on account of the rocky condition of the road.

"When one reaches the summit of the grade, an altitude of nearly 1,000 feet has been attained. The vista in all directions is wonderful. In the foreground, looking out

Montara Mountain

over the beautiful Pacific, is the strata-marked Point Pedro, now to the north of the motorists. The view of the ocean shore, its string of beaches and rocky points, extend as far as the eye can reach to both the north and south. Old Tamalpais, in Marin County, brings up the view to the north, but to the south the view fades away in the haze of distance.

"Treacherous as was the climb to the summit, the descent to the beaches on the south side of the ridge is even more so. One can not go down in a hurry, for if a single miscue does not result in a fatality or a serious accident, it is an act of providence. One of the grimmest spectacles along the road is the hole through the fence and the gash in the side of the mountain where the last machine went over the edge. It is a warning which the most daring will heed.

"After reaching the little hamlet of Montara, motorists will find comparatively smooth sailing all the way to Halfmoon Bay, from which place they may return to San Francisco by way of the Spring Valley Lakes road.

"From a scenic standpoint, this Call tour is unique. It is highly recommended to every motorist, but before starting out be sure your brakes will hold and that your car can climb. The journey calls for a 100 per cent efficiency car almost every moment, and a car with a short wheel base will have a much easier time of it than any other."

—March 17, 1912. *San Francisco Chronicle*

Crossings of Montara Mountain

Traces of the old Half Moon Bay–Colma Road switchback up the southern flank of San Pedro Mountain near the Saddle Cut and Devil's Slide promontory. In the early 1910s, as automobile excursions became more popular, San Mateo County was obliged to post "Dangerous for Automobiles" signs on the road. The Half Moon Bay–Colma Road was abandoned in 1917. Highway One curves at the base of the road cuts along the ocean bluffs.

Traces of the Half Moon Bay–Colma Road

In McNee Ranch State Park, take Gray Whale Cove Trail to hike part of the Half Moon Bay–Colma Road. This section of the road is as flat as a board. Look north across Green Valley to the Half Moon Bay–Colma Road cut on the south flank of San Pedro Mountain. It is lined with Pampas Grass.

Drive north on Highway One. After crossing Devil's Slide, the highway turns inland and descends to Pacifica. About midway, pull off the highway (legal pull-off). Shamrock Ranch lies below you. Across the valley, the old Half Moon Bay–Colma road winds down the hillside.

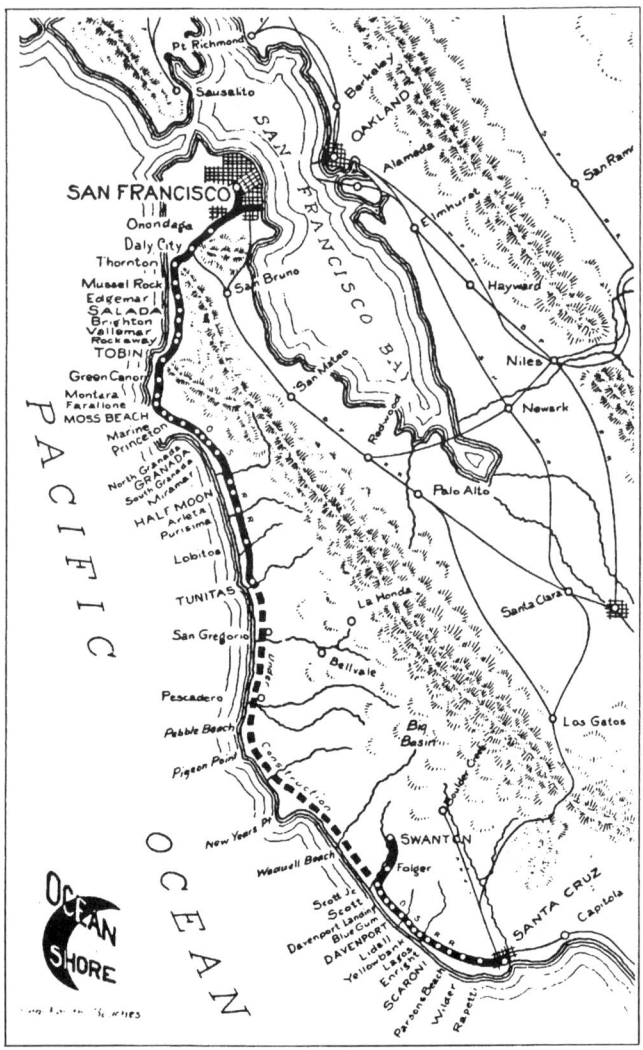

[Courtesy San Mateo County Historical Association]
Route of the Ocean Shore Railroad, 1907–1920.

Crossings of Montara Mountain

[Courtesy Will Whittaker]
An Ocean Shore Railroad passenger train crosses Devil's Slide "twixt sea and mountain."

Ocean Shore Railroad (1907–1920)

On October 2, 1907, San Pedro Mountain rang with the shrill whistle of the first Ocean Shore Railroad passenger train from San Francisco to Tobin station. A few months later, on May 28, 1908, the same whistle echoed off Montara Mountain as the first passenger train pulled into Montara station.

Between the two stations ran the most challenging four-mile crossing of the two mountains. Never before had anyone attempted going around them mid-way down the ocean bluffs. At the tip of Pedro Point, engineers blasted out a 354-foot tunnel. Along the "man-made ledge" at Devil's Slide, crews embedded steel pilings to hold up the roadbed. At the Saddle Cut south of Devil's Slide, they planted nine tons of black powder to blow off the top of a small mountain.

The Ocean Shore Railroad, with its slogan "Reaches the Beaches," intended to run between San Francisco and Santa Cruz but the roadbed was never finished. Passengers boarded a Stanley Steamer autobus to ride the twenty-six-mile gap between Tunitas, the last stop on the northern section of the line, and Swanton, the first stop on the southern section.

Within a few years, the increasing use of automobiles and trucks—and the commitment of taxpayer dollars to build roads—sounded the death knell for the Ocean Shore Railroad. When road crews couldn't keep the track open around San Pedro Mountain

Montara Mountain

[Courtesy California Department of Transportation]
1906. Building the Ocean Shore Railroad south of the Saddle Cut at Gray Whale Cove. Note the Half Moon Bay–Colma Road winding just above.

Today, Highway One uses the old Ocean Shore Railroad roadbed. Gray Whale Cove Trail in McNee Ranch State Park, just above Highway One, uses part of the old Half Moon Bay–Colma Road.

during winter storms, travellers took to their Fords, abandoning the Ocean Shore, and farmers loaded their artichokes onto trucks. The last scheduled train ran on August 16, 1920.

In the thirteen years the Ocean Shore Railroad ran, it changed the look of the San Mateo County coast forever.* San Francisco capitalists built the line to transport San Franciscans to blooming coastal resorts—and to sell them building lots. Over fifty-five suburban housing tracts were laid out along the route of the Ocean Shore, from Edgemar in northern Pacifica to Lobitos, south of Half Moon Bay. Even though only a few people settled on the coast, many of the tracts survived as communities. Today, on the North Coast, Pacifica is made up of Edgemar, Salada Beach and Brighton Beach (now known as Sharp Park), Vallemar, Rockaway Beach and Tobin (now known as Pedro Point)—all old Ocean Shore Railroad stops. On the Coastside, Montara, Moss Beach, Princeton, El Granada and Miramar are old suburban tracts.

Agriculture along the San Mateo County coast changed with the coming of the Ocean Shore. Farmers eagerly converted grain fields to vegetable gardens. Soon perishable crops of artichokes and peas, grown along the train track, began appearing on dinner tables across the country. Travellers on the train inevitably remarked on the acres and acres of artichokes which sped past their windows. When the Ocean Shore stopped running in 1920, over 95% of the country's artichokes were grown along the narrow coastal belt between San Pedro Valley and Santa Cruz.

Today, Highway One follows much of the route of the Ocean Shore Railroad through Pacifica, around Montara Mountain and along the Coastside until El Granada.

> **Names**
> The Ocean Shore Railroad named features along its route around San Pedro Mountain. None of the names stuck. Pedro Point became Roger's Point, after John B. Rogers, the engineer in charge of building the roadbed. We say "Devil's Slide"; the Ocean Shore said "San Pedro bluffs." We have no name for the massive cut at the south end of Devil's Slide; the Ocean Shore said both "Saddle Cut" and "Roger's Cut."

---

* For more on the Ocean Shore Railroad, see Barbara VanderWerf, *Granada, A Synonym for Paradise: The Ocean Shore Railroad Years*. 1992. Gum Tree Lane Books. El Granada, California.

Montara Mountain

[Courtesy San Mateo County Historical Association]
1908. Approaching Tobin station on Pedro Point. The Ocean Shore Railroad track curves around the shore, now Pacifica State Beach.

[Randolph Brandt Collection. Courtesy Tom Gray]
Tobin station (also known as San Pedro, San Pedro Terrace, San Pedro Terrace by the Sea, and Pedro Valley) served the new community on Pedro Point, the vegetable farmers of fertile Pedro Valley, and the many vacationers who enjoyed the nearby hotels, safe bathing beach and trout fishing in San Pedro Creek. The converted depot is now a private house (see page 12).

A Ride on the Ocean Shore Railroad

"The tourist finds new thrills upon entering San Pedro Valley, which seems as though it had been hewn from the base of one of the mountains of the great Coast Range. It is a charming spot. Though only three miles long by half a mile wide, every foot of its highly productive soil is under cultivation. Its produce is to be found on the tables of epicures the world over. The principle delicacy that thrives in this little valley is the artichoke, of which many carloads are shipped yearly to the markets of London and the Continent.

"Next is Tobin, formerly San Pedro Terrace, the shipping point for San Pedro Valley. Here the expectations of sportsmen with rod and reel are daily fulfilled, for at no place is there a more favored spot for surf fishing; from the speeding passenger car windows, fishermen are seen on cliffs, rocks and reefs, busily engaged in their fascinating vocation.

"Wonders on this Ocean Shore excursion never cease! Leaving Tobin, the railroad is built on great cliffs for several miles around Pedro Mountain, feats of engineering that amaze one. Far below, the tireless breakers dash with tremendous force against the cliffs, throwing great volumes of water skyward. Here we pass one of the most interesting objects of the trip, Point Rogers, a great rock of many colored strata, rivaling in beauty the world-renowned Rock of Gibraltar. Then comes the only tunnel on the line, which is broad and has a double track, bored through four hundred feet of solid rock.

"The eerie sensations experienced while riding around these few miles of bluff-built railway leave us when we swing in from the shore line for a short distance to enter a succession of deep rock cuts, after which come the rolling foothills of the Coast Range mountains and the resort cities of Montara, Farallone, Moss Beach and Marine View."

—Ocean Shore Railroad. 1913

Montara Mountain

[Courtesy The Bancroft Library]
A brave Ocean Shore train approaches the Saddle Cut on Devil's Slide. Nowadays, people celebrate the Ocean Shore Railroad as a delightful, rickety line that wound its way along the ocean bluffs to reach pleasant towns on the scenic San Mateo County coast.

Highway One and the Saddle Cut.

Another Ride on the Ocean Shore Railroad

"It is, you know—how do you say it?—'rococo,' that is the word.

"And, in passing, we might state that rococo is a very good word for use on special occasions. Such an occasion, for instance, as when excursioning over the Ocean Shore route—a stretch of country apparently decorated by a will-o'-the-wisp of fancy and fantasy for Nature's lair of grotesqueness… The Ocean Shore trails along dizzy, craggy heights of broken, beetle-browed bluffs overlooking the shimmering, placid waters of the Setting Sun…

"The five-coach train snakes along the man-made ledge, cut into the ragged, scowling promontories and fronting, sheer and awesomely, a limitless expanse of blue water. Looking down, one sees the ocean roll and break at its base as if bathing the feet of a giant in endless reverence of its mightiness. On our left is terra firma, on our right is more or less perpetual eternity.

"It is a trestle, a gap, a bluff and a jutting shoulder of earth, and then once again a trestle, and so on. In and out, following the belly of the broken mainland, bridging gorges and traversing miniature meadows, now staring into the scarred and serrated sides of the weather-ward cliffs, in and out, over and under, until the satiated mind becomes dizzy with the multiplicity of reflected visions."

—July 13, 1914. *Coast Side Comet*

Montara Mountain

[Courtesy Will Whittaker]

A northbound Ocean Shore train full of passengers near Green Valley. The Half Moon Bay–Colma Road (now Gray Whale Cove Trail in McNee Ranch State Park) runs above the track. Highway One uses the old railroad roadbed.

[Randolph Brandt Collection. Courtesy Tom Gray]

Montara depot had two-foot-thick walls made of Montara Mountain granite. Today, the remodeled depot is a private house on Second and Main in Montara.

And Another Ride on the Ocean Shore Railroad

" 'Pedro,' sang out the brakeman. And apparently we were at the end of the land, and maybe the world too. A great headland jutted into the ocean. But the train nosed its way safely around the first point, and there straight up toward heaven stood the mountain wall [San Pedro Mountain] and flat below lay the ocean stretched into limitless space, till sea and sky blended into the horizon of the world.

"Zip—we went into a tunnel, and out of it in almost no time, and then the country was too rough for townsites, but masses of yellow lupine spread their glory upon it [San Pedro Point tunnel and Devil's Slide]. It was a world for the geologist and the botanist to revel in.

" 'Green Canyon,' shouted the brakeman, and that was not a townsite but just an adorable little green dent in the straight up and downness of the land, where the train stopped to take on water for the engine. Then we swept around a magnificent curve and the whole scene changed. Far back, San Pedro Mountain stood full face to the ocean.

"A long reverberating whistle announced we were approaching Montara."

—Madge Morris Wagner. September 28, 1917. *Coast Side Comet*

Montara Mountain

[Randolph Brandt Collection. Courtesy Tom Gray]
1908. Ocean Shore train at Pedro Point. In the early years, flat bed cars were used to transport excursionists to the sandy beaches of the San Mateo County coast.

[Courtesy San Mateo County Historical Association]
Passengers and crew of an Ocean Shore train ponder what to do about the latest landslide on San Pedro Mountain.

More Rides on the Ocean Shore Railroad

"My mother and father rode the Ocean Shore many times, making the trip to Half Moon Bay to visit our relatives. Mother was very apprehensive on that part which traversed the cliffs, and where you could look down on the ocean. She would close her eyes, or many times change her seat to the other side of the coach to avoid looking down at the ocean."
—Vernon J. Sappers. September 6, 1992

"When we got to Devil's Slide, the track was gone. It'd been buried in a landslide. We had to get out of our passenger car and climb over the mud and boulders to get to a waiting train on the other side of the slide. My mother grabbed my hand and told me not to look down because we were walking along the edge just above the ocean."
—Rina Pacini. May 7, 1989

"After passing through the tunnel at San Pedro Point, the track virtually overhung the ocean. Once, a passenger train became trapped between a slide in front of it and one in back of it. It must have taken a person with nerve to climb over the slide to get help as it was obviously too steep to climb the two-or-three-hundred-foot cliff on the land side of the track."
—Malcolm Steel. October 29, 1956

Montara Mountain

[Courtesy San Mateo County Historical Association]
A puffing southbound Ocean Shore train accepts the salute of northbound Spaniards as they both cross Montara Mountain to open up new territories.

Crossings of Montara Mountain

Seven Paper Railroads over Montara Mountain
- **1881*** San Francisco and Ocean Shore Railroad (surveyed a route along the ocean bluffs of San Pedro Mountain and Montara Mountain)
- **1889** Pacific Railway Company
- **1892** Colma–Half Moon Bay Road (an electric line to run alongside the existing Half Moon Bay–Colma road)
- **1894** San Francisco and West Shore Railroad (a bogus company with no intentions to build)
- **1895** San Francisco and West Shore Railroad (later called West Shore Railroad. Planned to build a tunnel under the Saddle Pass between Green Valley and the valley of Willow Brook Estates in Pacifica.)
- **1903** San Francisco and Southern Railway Company
- **1905** Coast Line Railroad Company

The Only Railroad over Montara Mountain
- **1905** Ocean Shore Railroad

* Date of incorporation

Traces of the Ocean Shore Railroad

If you drive along Highway One, you can see quite a few traces of the Ocean Shore Railroad. Let Chapter 2, "A Drive Along Devil's Slide," be your guide.

In McNee Ranch State Park, hike Gray Whale Cove Trail, which runs above the old Ocean Shore roadbed. All the Highway One road cuts that you see below the trail were blasted out by Ocean Shore work crews in 1906.

At Gray Whale Cove parking lot, trains ran through the cut now spanned by a yellow gate. The route of the railroad joins the route of Highway One at the parking lot. Both continue south together until Martini Creek.

143

Montara Mountain

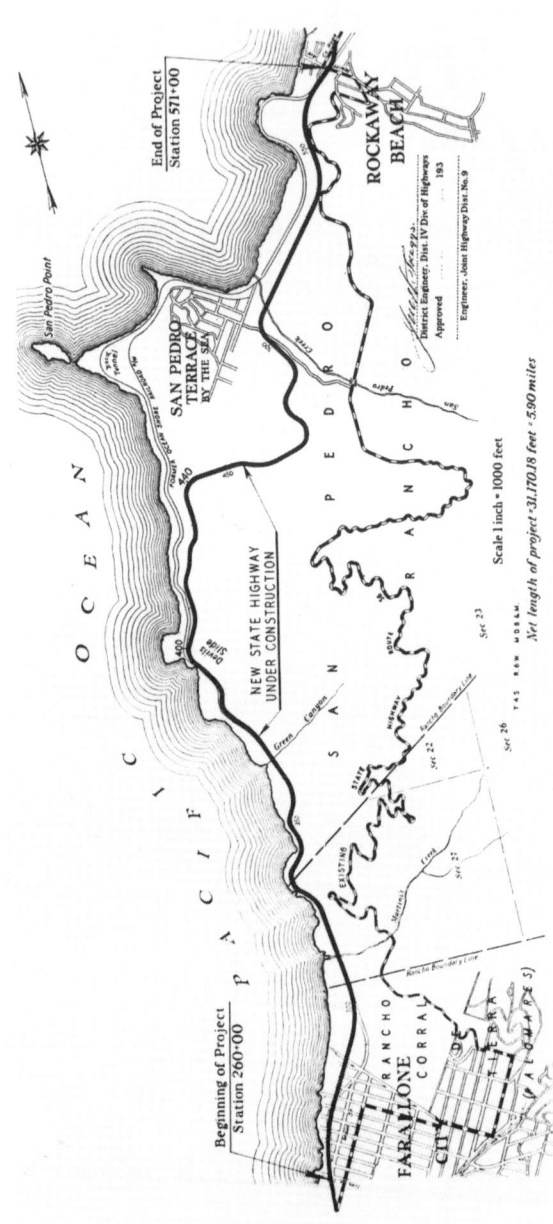

This 1937 map shows the Coastside Boulevard (renamed State Highway 56) as a dotted line snaking its way over Montara Mountain. The Coastside Boulevard used the Saddle Pass. Highway One, built to replace the Boulevard, is the dark line along the coast. The double line indicates the Ocean Shore Railroad right of way. Note the tunnel at the tip of Pedro Point.

[Courtesy California Department of Transportation]

" 'A woman needs to be very brave, or very much in love with her husband, who'll go with him on a trip over Montara Mountain,' said Mrs. Somebody to Mrs. Somebodyelse.
And Mrs. Somebodyelse said to Mrs. Somebody, 'Couldn't she be a bit of both?'
And Mrs. Somebody said, 'I never thought of that.' "
—September 1, 1916. *Coast Side Comet*

Coastside Boulevard (1915–1937)

By the early 1910s, everyone along the San Mateo County coast was clamoring for a new road. Most people had given up on the Ocean Shore Railroad, which could not keep its track open along Devil's Slide and could not run its trains on time. The Half Moon Bay–Colma Road had degenerated into a treacherous cow path. People were buying Fords in record numbers—and they needed good roads. County farmers needed to get their artichokes to San Francisco produce markets; San Francisco motorists wanted day trips along safe country roads; Coastside real estate promoters wanted to sell building lots to city folks; and Coastside hotel owners wanted vacationers to fill beds.

San Mateo County took quick action: the voters rousingly approved a bond issue for new roads; the county surveyor chose the Saddle Pass for the next crossing of Montara Mountain; and the County Supervisors hired a road builder. Base camp was at Martini Creek. From there, the contractor laid a railroad track, mounted a steam shovel to it, and dug out the new road to the Saddle Pass.

The Coastside Boulevard, which opened up the San Mateo County coast to auto-owning San Franciscans, was an instant success. On opening day, October 31, 1915, several thousand people made the trip over Montara Mountain, at each turn admiring the spectacular ocean and mountain views. On a sunny Sunday afternoon in 1916, four thousand cars jammed the twisting Boulevard, every driver required by law to honk his horn on each of the 250 curves in the road. Coastsiders, heady with the thoughts of prosperous days ahead, welcomed every car that came.

Montara Mountain

> "Go over that road and look at it. Every foot of it as even as the top of your table. Of course there is a gradual rise in it, all the way up, but it is so gradual that you can travel over it with an automobile as easily as if it were level; so straight and even are the lines of ascent that you will look at a stretch of a hundred or two hundred feet of it and say it is level, and yet there is a rise of six percent in most of it, and if you have ever driven a car you know that is a grade any car will take with the utmost ease. And the turns; they are so splendidly planned and executed that you can negotiate them with the same ease that you do the straight stretches; the road for hundreds of feet, yes, I think I am safe in saying for thousands of feet, is in plainest view ahead of you all the time and each of those turns gradually widens out as you approach it, and you find it a widened horseshoe, almost a perfect circle, instead of the old hairpin turn."
> —June 12, 1914. *Coast Side Comet*

Promoters of the Coastside Boulevard guaranteed that drivers could get from Montara to downtown San Francisco in thirty-five minutes. Of course, no driver did. The grade and turns over Montara Mountain were nearly impossible to navigate. Terrible accidents happened. The road surface, unable to bear heavily loaded artichoke trucks, rapidly disintegrated. The road drainage was never right: Landslides and washouts frequently closed the road. In 1920, five years after the Boulevard opened and when the Ocean Shore Railroad folded, Coastsiders, dissatisfied with the Saddle Pass crossing, agitated for a two-percent grade "Sea Level Boulevard" on the old Ocean Shore roadbed along the ocean face of the mountain. Today we call that route "Highway One."

The eighty-mile-long Coastside Boulevard (San Francisco to Santa Cruz) was part of the two-hundred-mile system of boulevards built in San Mateo County in the 1910s and 1920s. You can recognize these roads by their names: Skyline Boulevard, Junipero Serra Boulevard, Bay Shore Boulevard and Coastside Boulevard.

During the Prohibition years, rumrunners transported smuggled whiskey from foggy Coastside coves to San Francisco speak-easies over the twisty Coastside Boulevard.

Names
The Coastside Boulevard soon became known as San Pedro Mountain Road. Now it is called both Old San Pedro Mountain Road and Old Pedro Mountain Road.

Opening Day on the Coastside Boulevard

"The Coastside Boulevard was opened during the past week, and one of the first machines to pass over it was the Chronicle Studebaker pathfinding car, driven by Miss Helen Weaver, one of the most skilled drivers among California's women motorists. Each member of the pathfinding party immediately went on record saying that the boulevard would become one of the most popular motor pathways in the country. As the trip progressed, all became more convinced of the correctness of their predictions for the varying scenery, from wild-spraying surf to wonderfully cultivated truck gardens and panoramic views, all of which left most favorable impressions.

[The author describes the trip from Colma to San Pedro Valley.]

"At San Pedro Mountain, a 6% grade leads to the crest [Saddle Pass] from where a magnificent panoramic view of the Pacific Ocean and San Francisco Bay may be had. The view, coupled with the ease with which the point may be reached, makes the Colma–Half Moon Bay trip one of the banner trips of the west coast. From Montara to Halfmoon Bay, the road has a concrete base with an asphaltic oil surface. The entire road has a driving surface of sixteen feet, giving ample room for machines to pass and making the 'safety first' factor a prominent one."

—October 31, 1915 *San Francisco Chronicle*

"Every man who can scrape $500 together will be bundling his wife and children into the family flivver on Sunday mornings, and half the city will be off to the tune of 'A life on the ocean wave and a home on the ocean beach.' "

—November 19, 1915. *Coast Side Comet*

[Following pages:
 Photo top left: San Pedro Valley from San Pedro Mountain.
 Photo bottom left: San Pedro Valley.
 Photo top right: Montara and Montara Mountain.
 Photo bottom right: Rockaway Point.]

Automobile and Sporting News

VOL. CVII. SAN FRANCISCO

COLMA-HALFMOON BA

*Views along San Mateo county's new scenic boulevard between Colma and Halfmoon Bay, which pathway has just been opened to the
to negotiate the b*

NEW CAR ARRIVES, ATTRACTS DEAL OF ATTENTION

Reo "Six" Now on Display at Salesrooms of Earle C. Anthony, Inc.

"The new 1916 Reo Six has arrived in San Francisco. It has just been received by Earle C. Anthony, Inc. It is the finest looking Reo that has ever been turned out by R. E. Olds.

"In continuing the Reo Six for the coming year, refined and perfected at every point, the factory officials are not only giving Reo buyers the greatest value which is possible to obtain in a car of this size and type, but are also giving them the greatest guarantee of service and of satisfaction it is possible to have," says Hays "Speed" Eckert, resident manager.

"By far the most important change or improvement in this model over its predecessor is the body design, which is of the popular 'sheer-line' type.

"This type was originated by the famous Belgian, Vanden Plas, and has a tremendous international vogue. We think that the Reo designers have caught the spirit and

SAN MATEO'S NEWEST ROAD RICH IN SCENERY

Chronicle-Studebaker Pathfinders Predict New Path Skirting Ocean Shore Will Win Instant Popularity

By LEON J. PINKSON

SAN MATEO county has spent hundreds of thousands of dollars within the last year in building highways that have placed it on the map as one of the finest touring grounds to be found in any part of within reach of the Pacific. At others is high above the beach, winding s way through rich valleys, along side hills which have given fame to San Mateo county's truck gardens.

Miss Helen Weav the most skilled drivers who piloted The Chroni county's new ocean sho

Crossings of Montara Mountain

Chronicle

PAGES 43 to 50

DAY, OCTOBER 31, 1915.   NO. 108

HIGHWAY NOW OPEN

nd bids fair to become one of California's most famous touring grounds. The Chronicle-Studebaker pathfinding car, one of the first machines in the foreground.

1700 "FOREIGN" CARS VISIT CALIFORNIA

Seventeen hundred automobiles came into California from the East, North and South between the months of April and November of this year, according to the figures compiled by the Tourist Association of Central California. Of this number 794 came over the Lincoln Highway and registered at Ely, Nev., and 205 turned west at Ogden and followed the railroad line to Reno. More than 400 cars came into California from Oregon and 105 cars entered the State from Arizona.

Of the 794 cars which registered at Ely, Nev., more than a third, or 265, were diverted south via Goldfield to Los Angeles, and 529 came west via Carson or Reno. Although an effort was made to have all cars register at Ely, Nev., it is thought a larger number, possibly 200, failed to do so, and the actual number is therefore greater than the available figures show.

The total does not include automobiles shipped into California and later used for touring. Allowing 15 per cent for these and others that slipped in without registering at points of entry, the Tourist Association gives the number of "foreign" cars visiting California for the six months at 1727 and the probable number of passengers, at four per car, at 6908.

Yosemite valley was visited by 2350 private automobiles up to October 25th, as against 739 last year, an increase of more than 200 per cent in motor travel to the valley over 1914. Of the 32,000 visitors to Yosemite valley this season, about one-third traveled by automobiles.

SCRIPPS-BOOTH CAR A WINNER HERE

Gus A. Boyer, sales manager of the John F. McLain Company, Northern California distributors of the Franklin and Scripps-Booth lines, is at present visiting in the East visiting the two factories which his firm represents. Boyer's mission is primarily to hear shipments of both makes of cars. He will spend some days in Detroit at the Scripps-Booth plant before going to the Franklin factory at Syracuse.

Since the McLain Company accepted the appointment as distributors of the Scripps-Booth line the officials of the firm have been kept busy making demonstrations with the attractive little roadster, and the way orders have been booked it was necessary for Boyer to hasten East and get shipments started.

The Scripps-Booth line is a small, luxuriously finished car, not built to compete in the cheap-price class, but for the purpose of providing a small light car that might be used by the owner of larger models for individual purposes. The car is well constructed, has a wealth of power and, according to the McLain Company officials, is just the machine for work in and about the city.

In addition to the roadster, the factory is building a light coupe that is meeting with huge success in the East among society women, who are using this enclosed model for shopping and social purposes. The first of these models is expected to arrive here shortly.

. N. Weaver, and one of
california women motorists,
finding car over San Mateo

JUST ARRIVED
Come and See the
SAXON "SIX"

Montara Mountain

[Courtesy California Department of Transportation]

1930s. The Coastside Boulevard winding down into Montara. The State Division of Highways took over the road in 1933, numbering it State Highway 56. It reverted back to the County when present-day Highway One opened in 1937. The County abandoned the road after World War II.

Today you can hike the Coastside Boulevard, now called Old Pedro Mountain Road, in McNee Ranch State Park and marvel that it was once promoted as a road any car could drive with ease.

[Courtesy Ted Wurm]

1926. A caravan of artichoke trucks sets off from Half Moon Bay for San Francisco. Such caravans quickly destroyed the macadamized (crushed gravel sealed with oil) surface of the Coastside Boulevard over Montara Mountain.

More Drives on the Coastside Boulevard

> "I've seen many crooked things in my time, but the Boulevard from San Francisco is about the crookedest piece of road I've ever run across."
> —August 25, 1915. *Coast Side Comet*

> "The road over Montara Mountain got so foggy that sometimes my grandmother had to walk ahead of the car with a lantern to find the way. We kids hated that road. We crouched in the back of the car and still got sick."
> —Norma Muniz. March 15, 1991

> "When we traveled [from San Francisco] to the beach on Sundays between 1925 and 1932, it was by the terrible winding road over Pedro Mountain, *a guaranteed source of car sickness.*"
> —Ted Wurm. January 12, 1991

Montara Mountain

[Courtesy San Mateo County Historical Association]
1916. The Coastside Boulevard around the rim of Green Valley. The Saddle Pass is to the left. Building the two-lane, sixteen-foot-wide road caused an enormous amount of devastation.

Seventy-five years later, the Coastal Scrub plant community has reasserted itself: The scars are overgrown with native vegetation. Nowadays, any scars are quickly colonized by Pampas Grass, which was introduced by Caltrans in the 1960s for erosion control along Highway One (in the foreground).

Crossings of Montara Mountain

Bus Lines over Montara Mountain (1915–1937)

[Randolph Brandt Collection. Courtesy Tom Gray]
Red Star Stage Line, San Francisco to Pescadero, 1914–1922.

Coastside Transport Company, San Francisco to Pescadero, 1921–1937.

[Courtesy Bob Burrowes]

Traces of the Coastside Boulevard

Hike Old Pedro Mountain Road in McNee Ranch State Park to enjoy the magnificent sweeping views and six percent grade which made the Coastside Boulevard famous. Near the Ranger's residence look for the Martini Creek bridge foundations. If you look carefully along the trail, you might spot a few rickety old guard rails.

Montara Mountain

[Courtesy California Department of Transportation]

1937. Highway One was open to traffic on Armistice Day, November 11, 1937. South from the Saddle Cut (shown above) to Martini Creek the highway uses the roadbed of the Ocean Shore Railroad. The highway builders were especially proud of the numerous view pull-offs, which were banked by parapets made from Montara Mountain rock. The Half Moon Bay–Colma Road runs above the highway. See page 144 for a map of Highway One.

[Courtesy Louie Bertolucci]
1950s. Montara Mountain looms behind Frank Torres Restaurant, a popular stop for travellers along Highway One. Today, diners at the Chart House enjoy the same view.

Highway One (1937–present)

The Ocean Shore Railroad was no more. On August 16, 1920, the last passenger train puffed its way north to San Francisco across the face of Devil's Slide. A scant mile inland, automobiles and artichoke trucks ground their way along the disintegrating Coastside Boulevard. Residents up and down the San Mateo County coast predicted glum economic times ahead. With the train gone and the treacherous Boulevard falling apart, how would San Franciscans get to Coastside restaurants and sandy beaches, and how would Coastside artichokes get to San Franciscans?

In the early 1920s, Coastsiders made a decision that was to affect us to this day: Rather than fix the Coastside Boulevard over the Saddle Pass, they chose to fix the roadbed of the Ocean Shore Railroad around San Pedro Mountain. They proposed the "Sea Level Boulevard," with a grade of two percent, through the 354-foot tunnel at Pedro Point, across the man-made ledge at Devil's Slide, and through the Saddle Cut. Even though the entrance to the tunnel had been blasted shut by Prohibition agents (to prevent rumrunners from caching their whiskey), everyone agreed that the tunnel would be perfect for a new highway.

Just as the Ocean Shore Railroad hoped to link three counties—San Francisco, San Mateo and Santa Cruz—so did the

Montara Mountain

1920s–1930s. The railroad track is gone; only a footpath threads through the Saddle Cut. Today, Highway One uses the old Ocean Shore Railroad Saddle Cut.

[Courtesy Louie Bertolucci]

Letter to the San Mateo County Board of Supervisors, 1924

"It is painful to contemplate the blight that fell upon the west strip of the county when the railroad failed and was removed. The steep and dangerous grade of the Coastside Boulevard requires too much gas to lift cars and trucks over its elevation, and takes too much time. The hundreds of ruined little places along the coastline indicate the despair the owners felt of any relief by the Boulevard. No county official with the interest of his people at heart can neglect any legitimate means of attracting settlers. And no class of settlers is more an asset than those people whose material conditions are such that they can lift their homeseeking eyes to regions of health and beauty. San Mateo County can offer these in abundance. With this strip of coast in its highway system [the Sea Level Boulevard], San Mateo County would outshine any other in the world."

proposed seventy-five-mile-long highway. In 1928, the three counties formed Joint Highway District Number 9, which with state and federal help, built our present-day Highway One. San Francisco County agreed to pay 55% of the costs even though only two miles of the new road were within its boundaries. After all, pleasure-loving San Franciscans benefited from a quick, easy way to the beaches and they ate well on superior, rapidly-transported San Mateo County produce. San Mateo County, with fifty-nine miles in its boundaries, agreed to pay 30%; Santa Cruz County, with fourteen miles, agreed on 15%.

The Ocean Shore Railroad relinquished most of its right of way—except for the three mile section from Tobin on Pedro Point to the Saddle Cut. It argued that maybe the railroad would start up again—or maybe somebody else would buy the line and need the tunnel. Also, it claimed to have invested nearly a million dollars in blasting the tunnel through Pedro Point and in carving out a ledge along Devil's Slide. If the highway builders agreed to pay the railroad for its troubles, then the new Sea Level Boulevard could use the tunnel. If not, then the highway builders would have to find another way across San Pedro Mountain.

> "Is there no other way to get past Pedro Point? To the motorcar, a few hundred yards more of distance on a bit of well-laid-out grade means nothing. Portolá's men got past Pedro Point without climbing around the face of a cliff. And it did not cost them one hundred thousand pesos. A modern highway engineer ought to be able to do as well as Portolá, who probably didn't even have a transit."
> —June 21, 1932. *San Francisco Chronicle*

For the Pedro Point route, the Ocean Shore asked $1,000,000. The court decided that $112,000 was a fair price. The highway builders countered with $25,000 and began condemnation proceedings. The Ocean Shore appealed. The squabbling continued until 1935, when the highway builders gave up and their surveyors staked out a new route behind Pedro Point and above the railroad right of way on Devil's Slide. We drive that route today.

The Sea Level Boulevard through the tunnel was no more.

Montara Mountain

[Courtesy California Department of Transportation]
1937. Highway One looking south at the Pedro Point intersection. The highway goes inland behind Pedro Point. Artichoke fields fill Pedro Valley. Montara Mountain is in the background.

1994. Highway One at the Pedro Point intersection south of Linda Mar veers left to begin the climb behind Pedro Point. If the Ocean Shore Railroad had relinquished the tunnel through Pedro Point, we would veer right to drive around Shelter Cove and through the tunnel. Montara Mountain is in the background. Compare the two routes by looking at the map on page 144.

Crossings of Montara Mountain

[Courtesy California Department of Transportation]
1937. Highway One looking north at the Pedro Point intersection. The old Ocean Shore Railroad dike runs along the shore. San Pedro Creek, marked by the white guard rails, flows under the highway to the ocean.

[Courtesy California Department of Transportation]
1937. Looking north on Highway One behind Pedro Point. Sweeney Ridge and San Pedro Valley are in the background.

Montara Mountain

[Courtesy California Department of Transportation]
1937. Building Highway One at Devil's Slide.

Road construction on Highway One began in 1935. Building the roadbed proved as much of a challenge to highway engineers with powerful modern equipment as it had to railroad engineers with horse-drawn equipment.

> "The location of the highway along the cliff face required men with the agility of mountain goats, courage, experience, and complete lack of nerves. One false step meant a tumble into the breakers. The contractor's pioneering operations in this area are an epic in themselves. To launch 15-ton cats into space and carve a precarious foothold in the cliffs could be entrusted only to a few specially skilled and daring cat skinners. That this work was safely accomplished, with only one serious injury, is a tribute to the skill and daring of the men and contractor. On several occasions shovels, cats and compressors were covered by great slides, but only one worker was injured."
> —June, 1937. *California Highways and Public Works*

The fills presented more problems than the cuts: One fill was first excavated forty feet below grade and then rebuilt to grade by anchoring large rocks to the mountainside. In all, 700,000 cubic yards of dirt were moved at Devil's Slide. For the total 5.9 mile section from Rockaway Beach to Montara, one-and-one-half million cubic yards were moved. The engineers were especially proud of the pull-offs guarded by parapets made from Montara Mountain rock. Some of the parapets still exist.

Between Rockaway Beach and Montara, the new 5.9-mile section of Highway One was a great improvement over the old 10.6-mile section of the Coastside Boulevard. Highway One has 28 curves; the Coastside Boulevard had 250 curves. Highway One, on the Pacifica side, climbs 1.2 miles to reach its highest point of 465 feet; the Boulevard climbed 3 miles to its highest point of 922 feet at the Saddle Pass. Highway One is 26 feet wide; the Boulevard was only 16 feet wide. The Boulevard was known as the most dreaded travel route in the Bay Area; Highway One became known as the most scenic. The 5.9 mile section cost $578,815 to build.

Once the highway opened, developers—especially in El Granada—began sharpening their pencils in anticipation of a building boom. Farmers planted more sugar beets, which had replaced artichokes as the big cash crop, and hotel and restaurant owners, hoping for a rush of tourists, gussied up their buildings. But none of these folks were allowed to advertise along the new highway. In 1936, San Mateo County zoned Highway One a scenic route: No billboards or hot dog stands were allowed.

[Courtesy California Department of Transportation]
1937. Highway One, Devil's Slide and the Saddle Cut.

Montara Mountain

In 1937, motorists drove over the new highway as enthusiastically as they had driven over the Coastside Boulevard in 1915, twenty-two years earlier, and as they had ridden the first Ocean Shore trains in 1908, twenty-nine years earlier. Each new road promised growth and prosperity to the land north and south of Montara Mountain. Each road promised San Franciscans an easy access to their rightful playgrounds along Pacific Ocean beaches. But within a few years, each new road was dismissed as unsatisfactory. In April of 1940, a few years after Highway One opened, a huge slide at Devil's Slide dumped much of the concrete road into the surf below. Earlier, the State Division of Highways had commented,

> "It is anticipated that considerable trouble will be experienced by our maintenance forces during the next two or three winters, in keeping the roadway clear of minor slides and the natural sloughing of material from the steep mountain slopes."
> —December, 1937. *California Highways and Public Works*

[Courtesy California Department of Transportation]
The distinctive silhouettes of San Pedro Mountain and San Pedro Rock beckon the lone motorist on the Thornton (Daly City)—Edgemar (Pacifica) stretch of Highway One. This section, on the roadbed of the Ocean Shore Railroad, opened in 1936 and closed in 1957 after an earthquake. You can walk bits of the old highway, although most of it has fallen into the ocean. You can also see the old roadbed along the bluff face from nearly every vantage point on Montara Mountain.

Bus Lines over Montara Mountain (1937–present)

In 1993, members of the Pacific Bus Museum took a sentimental journey on the Greyhound bus which used to travel Highway One between San Francisco and Half Moon Bay.

Silver-sided Greyhound busses, decorated with the sleek greyhound dog, plied Highway One between 1937 and 1976. The "O" bus ran between San Francisco and Half Moon Bay; the "N" bus between San Francisco and Linda Mar in Pacifica.

In 1976, SamTrans took over the Greyhound routes. Today you can ride 1L and 1C between San Francisco, Pacifica and Half Moon Bay.

If you are lucky, you may spot a Green Tortoise bus, a relic of the sixties, which still makes occasional scheduled runs along Highway One.

Names
Highway One has gone by three names:
- Ocean Shore Highway, after the Ocean Shore Railroad,
- Coast Highway,
- Cabrillo Highway, after Spain's Juan Rodríguez Cabrillo, who sailed the California coast in 1542.

Montara Mountain

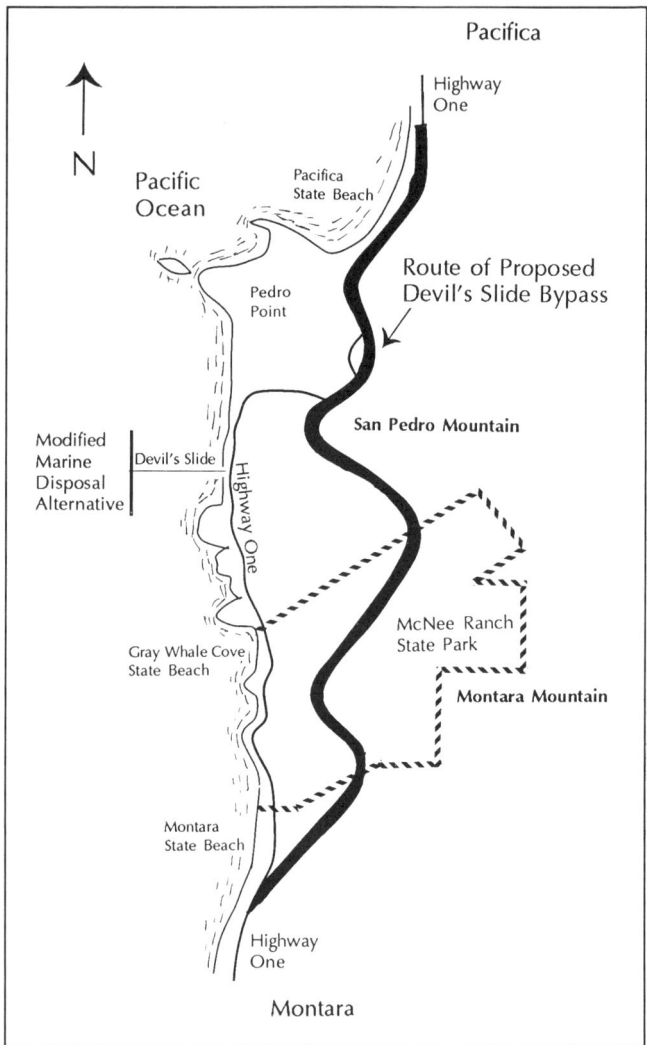

Highway One and the proposed Devil's Slide Bypass over Montara Mountain. Many lovers of the San Mateo County coast want to keep the ocean bluff crossing (Highway One). Caltrans wants to abandon the ocean bluff crossing for the Saddle Pass crossing (Devil's Slide Bypass).

In the past, people along the San Mateo County coast danced in the streets at the announcement of each new crossing of Montara Mountain. Whether along the ocean bluffs or over the Saddle Pass, each crossing promised growth and prosperity to Coastsiders. The environmental costs were never considered. Nowadays, for many people, growth is not a virtue, while respecting the environment is. Not everyone dances in the streets at the thought of the Devil's Slide Bypass.

Modified Marine Disposal Alternative or Devil's Slide Bypass

The Problem
If you have driven Devil's Slide on Highway One, you know that something has to be done. The yellow warning signs between the two S-curves mark off 1,000 feet of highway which is obviously deteriorating. One wet winter could saturate the slope above, cause it to fail and slump on the highway below. The question is, should we fix a 1,000-foot problem with a 1,000-foot solution or with a 4.5-mile solution?

The Proposals
The **Modified Marine Disposal Alternative**[1] involves moving 1,000 feet of highway to stable rock just 250 feet inland. The rock excavated from the bluff would be used to strengthen the highway bench. This plan requires one cut and one fill. Estimated cost is under $12 million. The Modified Marine Disposal Alternative meets the California Coastal Act requirement that scenic Highway One remain two lanes in rural areas.

The **Devil's Slide Bypass**[2] (officially called the Martini Creek Alternative) involves building a 4.5-mile highway over the Saddle Pass nearly a mile inland. It would require eight cuts and four fills. The Saddle Pass cut would be 250 feet deep. (Pillar Point—the dish-antenna-covered promontory near Princeton—would fit nicely into the Saddle Pass cut.) Each of the other cuts would be over 150 feet deep. The fills would be between 200 and 300 feet high. The steep Bypass—at a 6.5% grade—would require a downhill vehicle recovery lane (for runaway vehicles) and an uphill passing lane for a total of three (in places four) lanes. This plan stretches the intent of the Coastal Act to keep Highway One two lanes. Estimated cost is $100 million, of which Caltrans has $47 million.

---

[1] The Modified Marine Disposal Alternative is proposed by the Sierra Club and the Committee for Permanent Repair of Highway One. Joined by the Committee for Green Foothills and Shamrock Ranch, these are the four plaintiffs in the ongoing court action concerning the Devil's Slide Bypass.

Caltrans studied a Marine Disposal Alternative which would have moved 4,300 feet of Highway One just inland from the present alignment. It rejected the plan as too expensive. The Modified Marine Disposal Alternative is a scaled down—and cheaper—version. Caltrans has not studied it.

[2] The Devil's Slide Bypass is proposed by Caltrans, the defendant in ongoing court action.

Montara Mountain

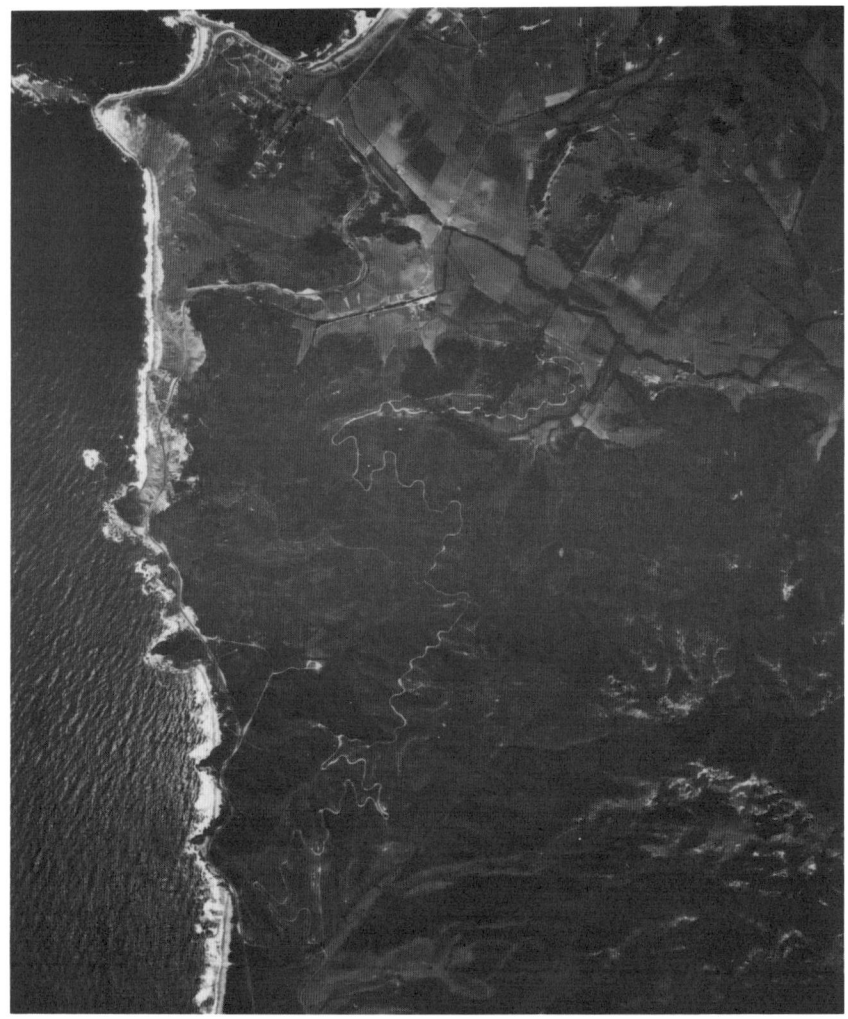

[Courtesy U. S. Geological Survey]

In this 1946 aerial, the crossings of Montara Mountain look pretty much as they do today: The Coastside Boulevard snakes across the Saddle Pass, intersecting the thread-like Road Trail; the Half Moon Bay–Colma Road scallops along the bluffs at Devil's Slide; the Ocean Shore Railroad's man-made ledge clings to Pedro Point; and Highway One joins the railroad roadbed at the Saddle Cut.

Other than for these crossings, Montara Mountain bears few man-made scars. The proposed 4.5-mile-long Devil's Slide Bypass would roughly follow the route of the Coastside Boulevard (except for the loop around the valley of Shamrock Ranch), but it would be six times as wide and would be banked with colossal cuts and fills. The Modified Marine Disposal Alternative would move 1,000 feet of Highway One just 250 feet inland.

Crossing Montara Mountain

A Bit of Background

The proposed Bypass is a relic of the late 1950s, when San Francisco developers cast their eyes on the San Mateo County coast. Andrew Oddstad staked out the Linda Mar district of Pacifica. Henry Doelger, the builder of the Sunset District of San Francisco and the Westlake District of Daly City, staked out 7,000 acres between Montara Mountain and El Granada. Doelger foresaw 60,000 home seekers spilling over Montara Mountain to his proposed suburban tracts. All he needed was a six-lane freeway over the mountain—and Caltrans agreed to build one. Doelger soon disappeared, but the Devil's Slide Bypass remained on the map. As Highway One deteriorated at Devil's Slide, Caltrans dusted off its plan, scaled it down a bit, and prepared to fire up the bulldozers.

But times have changed. People of the urban Bay Area value pristine Montara Mountain and the rural Coastside. Many question the need for carving up a mountain to pour more people onto fragile coastal terraces. As of this writing, the Bypass issue is still in the courts.

The Concerns

Fog: If you have driven Devil's Slide on a foggy day, chances are you drove through a fog tunnel. Fog tends to roll up the ocean bluffs, leaving clear visibility on the highway.

If you have driven Highway One at Skyline Boulevard (a few miles north between Pacifica and Daly City) on a foggy day, you know that fog settles on the highway and visibility can be near zero. The Saddle Pass, where the Devil's Slide Bypass intends to cross Montara Mountain, is just as foggy as Skyline Boulevard, if not worse. The Coastside Boulevard used the Saddle Pass between 1915 and 1937. Oldtimers recall how passengers would often get out of their cars to lead the drivers over the Pass in heavy fogs.

Safety: Highway One across Devil's Slide has a remarkable safety record for a two-lane highway, consistently registering fewer accidents than the average for similar highways in the Bay Area. However, accidents at Devil's Slide get a lot of press.

The Devil's Slide Bypass, on the other hand, would be a very steep road (6.5% grade) across a very foggy mountain pass.

Highway closures: Highway One at Devil's Slide has been open 98.6% of the time over its fifty-seven-year lifespan. In 1983, landslides closed the highway for 84 days. Caltrans improved the drainage and the highway has been open ever since. Engineering geologists testify that the slope problem at Devil's Slide can be permanently—and cheaply—repaired to prevent landslides.

167

Montara Mountain

Environment: The Modified Marine Disposal Alternative involves dumping rock debris into the ocean. Marine biologists, including Caltrans's, testify that damage to aquatic life would be minimal.

The Devil's Slide Bypass would destroy several hundred acres of Coastal Scrub, already a threatened plant community in the Bay Area. Caltrans admits that it would be able to revegetate native plants on only 10% of the cut-and-fill slopes. Biologists predict Pampas Grass would colonize the remaining 90% of the slopes.

Look on page 152 to see the devastation caused when the sixteen-foot-wide, two-lane Coastside Boulevard was built in 1915. The ninety-one-foot-wide, three-to-four-lane Devil's Slide Bypass would run just below the old road. Huge fills would cascade down the side of Green Valley to the valley floor. The Saddle Pass would be lowered 250 feet. These cuts and fills, far more massive than those for the Coastside Boulevard, would never revegetate with native plants.

Building on the ocean bluffs is never a good idea. However, carving up a pristine mountain for a new 4.5-mile-long highway is not a good idea either. Of the two choices, the Modified Marine Disposal Alternative would cause less environmental damage.

McNee Ranch State Park: Devil's Slide Bypass would bisect McNee Ranch State Park. Every hike would be accompanied by the sight and sound of roaring vehicles. Trails would use highway underpasses, as would migrating animals. The park would no longer be a serene island for Bay Area residents.

Scenic values: On the Pacifica side of Montara Mountain, the cuts and fills required for the Devil's Slide Bypass would be visible from as far as Marin County. To imagine the visual impact, expand your present-day view of the overgrown Old Pedro Mountain Road (the Coastside Boulevard), which has fifteen-foot-high road cuts, into the Devil's Slide Bypass, which would have 200-to-300-foot-high cuts and fills. Someone once said that if Caltrans threatened to carve up Mt. Tamalpais in Marin County with such a colossal highway, the Bay Area would unite in revolt. Montara Mountain deserves the same respect.

Conclusion

Highway One along Devil's Slide is a Bay Area scenic treasure. It can be permanently repaired to give travellers a safe and inspirational drive. The alternative—a 4.5-mile inland highway—would forever destroy pristine Montara Mountain and the rural San Mateo County coast, which Bay Area residents cherish.

Helpful Books

Plants and Wildlife
Berry, William D. and Elizabeth. 1959. *Mammals of the San Francisco Bay Region.* University of California Press. Berkeley, California.
Ferris, Roxana S. 1968. *Native Shrubs of the San Francisco Bay Region.* University of California Press. Berkeley, California.
Grillos, Steve J. 1966. *Ferns and Fern Allies of California.* University of California Press. Berkeley, California.
Ingles, Lloyd G. 1965. *Mammals of the Pacific States.* Stanford University Press. Stanford, California.
Le Boeuf, Burney J. and Stephanie Kaza. 1981. *The Natural History of Año Nuevo.* Boxwood Press. Pacific Grove, California.
Lyons, Kathleen and Mary Beth Cooney-Lazaneo. 1988. *Plants of the Coast Redwood Region.* Looking Press. Boulder Creek, California.
Niehaus, Theodore F. 1976. *A Field Guide to Pacific States Wildflowers.* Houghton Mifflin Company. Boston, Massachusetts.
Raiche, Roger. 1986. Testimony. *Final Environmental Impact Statement: Devil's Slide Bypass.* California Department of Transportation. Sacramento, California.
Robbins, Chandler S., Bertel Bruun, and Herbert S. Zim. 1966. *Birds of North America.* Golden Press. New York, New York.
Sharsmith, Helen K. 1970. *Spring Wildflowers of the San Francisco Bay Region.* University of California Press. Berkeley, California.
Stebbins, Robert C. 1971. *Reptiles and Amphibians of the San Francisco Bay Region.* University of California Press. Berkeley, California.
Thomas, John Hunter. 1961. *Flora of the Santa Cruz Mountains of California.* Stanford University Press. Stanford, California.
Williams, John C. and Howard C. Monore. 1970. *A Field Guide to the Natural History of the San Francisco Bay Area.* McCutchan Publishing. Berkeley, California.

Ocean Shore Railroad
VanderWerf, Barbara. 1992. *Granada, A Synonym for Paradise: The Ocean Shore Railroad Years.* Gum Tree Lane Books. El Granada, California.

Sources quoted
Burcham, Levi T. 1957. *California Rangeland: An Historico-ecological Study of the Range Resources of California.* Department of Natural Resources. Sacramento, California.
Chase, J. Smeaton. 1913. *California Coast Trails: A horseback ride from Mexico to Oregon.* Reprint 1987. Tioga Publishing Company. Palo Alto, California.
Gordon, Burton L. 1985. *Monterey Bay Area: Natural History and Cultural Imprints.* Boxwood Press. Pacific Grove, California.
Lawson, Andrew C. 1908. *The California Earthquake of April 18, 1906.* Carnegie Institution of Washington. Washington, D.C.
McGowan, Edward. 1946. *McGowan vs. California Vigilants.* Biobooks. Oakland, California.
Stanger, Frank M. and Alan K. Brown. 1969. *Who Discovered the Golden Gate?* San Mateo County Historical Association. San Mateo, California.

Plant Index

Alum Root	81	Douglas Iris	89
Beach Sagewort	74	Douglas Nightshade	63
Beach Strawberry	63	Dwarf Coyote Bush	69
Bird's Foot Lotus	76	Farewell-to-Spring	79
Bleeding Heart	82	Fat Solomon's Seal	65
Blue Dicks	89	Fetid Adder's Tongue	86
Blue Elderberry	93	Field Chickweed	62
Blue Gum Eucalyptus	58, 96	Field Mustard	72
Blue Witch	88	Flax	87
Blue-eyed Grass	88	Flowering Currant	84
Bluff Lettuce	78	Footsteps of Spring	75
Bracken Fern	99	Fragrant Everlasting	66
Bull Thistle	84	Franciscan Paintbrush	83
Bush Lupine	76	Franciscan Wallflower	73
California Bee Plant	83	Fringe Cups	81
California Blackberry	61	Fuller's Teasel	85
California Buttercup	73	Giant Trillium	79
California Coast Delphinium	92	Giant Vetch	83
California Coast Phacelia	89	Golden Back Fern	100
California Hazelnut	85	Golden Chinquapin	95
California Lilac	92	Goldenrod	75
California Maidenhair Fern	100	Gum Plant	73
California Milkwort	82	Hairy Honeysuckle	84
California Polypody	100	Hedge Nettle	91
California Poppy	72	Henderson's Angelica	66
California Wax Myrtle	94	Himalaya Berry	61
Coast Aster	90	Hound's Tongue	88
Coast Barberry	77	Huckleberry	70
Coast Buckwheat	65	Ithuriel's Spear	89
Coast Gooseberry	85	Lady Fern	100
Coast Live Oak	96	Lizard Tail	75
Coast Madia	74	Madrone	94
Coast Paintbrush	83	Manzanita	71
Coast Rock Cress	79	Meadow Rue	77
Coast Sagebrush	69	Milkmaids	62
Coast Silktassel	95	Miner's Lettuce	65
Coast Sun Cup	72	Mission Bells	86
Coast Trillium	62	Montara Manzanita	71
Coastal Wood Fern	99	Monterey Cypress	58, 97
Cobweb Thistle	84	Monterey Pine	58, 97
Coffee Berry	69	Mugwort	68
Common Wallflower	73	Pacific Sanicle	75
Cow Parsnip	66	Pacific Starflower	80
Coyote Bush	69	Pampas Grass	59, 101
Coyote Mint	91	Pearly Everlasting	66
Cream Bush	71	Periwinkle	88
Creek Dogwood	93	Pitcher Sage	68
Douglas Fir	98	Poison Hemlock	67

Wildlife Index

Poison Oak	61
Rattlesnake Grass	101
Red Alder	96
Red Elderberry	93
Redwood	98
Rosilla	74
Salal	81
Scarlet Pimpernel	80
Sea Pink	81
Seaside Daisy	90
Skunkweed	91
Slim Solomon's Seal	64
Snowberry	70
Soap Plant	63
Sow Thistle	74
Star Lily	64
Sticky Cinquefoil	63
Sticky Monkey Flower	76
Stinging Nettle	86
Stinging Phacelia	67
Stonecrop	78
Sweet Alyssum	65
Thimbleberry	70
Toyon	94
Twinberry	77
Varicolored Lupine	90
Western Chain Fern	100
Western Columbine	82
Western Dog Violet	87
Western Morning Glory	67
Western Sword Fern	99
White Globe Lily	62
Wild Cucumber	67
Wild Hollyhock	80
Wild Oats	101
Wild Radish	87
Wild Rose	80
Wild Sweet Pea	82
Willows	95
Wood Orchid	64
Woolly Sunflower	73
Yarrow	68
Yerba Buena	68
Yerba Santa	92

Mammals
Bobcat	105
Brush Rabbit	106
Coyote	104
Gray Fox	104
Merriam Chipmunk	105
Mountain Lion	105
Mule Deer	106
Opossum	106
Pocket Gopher	105
Raccoon	104
Striped Skunk	104
Wood Rat	30, 106

Lizards
Alligator Lizard	107
Fence Lizard	107

Molluscs
Banana Slug	107

Birds
American Kestrel	108
Anna's Hummingbird	109
Bewick's Wren	111
Black Phoebe	110
Brown Towhee	112
Bushtit	111
California Quail	109
California Thrasher	112
Chickadee	111
House Finch	113
House Sparrow	113
Mourning Dove	109
Oregon Junco	113
Raven	109
Red-shafted Flicker	110
Red-tailed Hawk	108
Robin	112
Rufous-sided Towhee	112
Scrub Jay	110
Song Sparrow	113
Starling	112
Stellar's Jay	110
Turkey Vulture	108
White-crowned Sparrow	113
Winter Wren	111
Wrentit	111

Subject Index

Subject Index

American ranchers 13, 37, 51, 56, 121
Brooks Creek Trail 30
Brooks Falls Overlook Trail 29
Bunkers 21, 22, 43, 46, 47
Busses 153, 163
Coastal Chaparral 54
Coastal Scrub 17, 54-56, 167
Coastside (name) 9
Coastside Boulevard 47, 144-153, 161
Costanos 23, 36, 56, 116
Devil's Slide 16, 17, 19-20, 21, 23, 131, 133, 160
Devil's Slide Bypass 7, 51, 165-168
Doelger, Henry 43, 166
Geology 17-18, 20, 46
Gray Whale Cove Trail 22, 41-44
Gray Whales 42
Green Valley 18, 42-43, 44, 138 152, 167
Guerrero–Palomares, Francisco 119
Half Moon Bay–Colma Road 16, 17, 22, 44, 122-129, 132, 154
Hazelnut Trail 35
Highway One 18, 19, 42, 44, 133, 143, 146, 154-163, 165-168
Indian Trail 116, 121
Martini Creek 23, 46, 116
McNee, Duncan 51
McNee Ranch State Park 39, 51, 167
Mexicans 37, 119-120
Modified Marine Disposal 165-168
Montara Depot 131, 138
Montara Knob 50
Montara Mountain (name) 9
Montara Mountain Trail 31-32, 49
Montara State Beach 23
North Coast (name) 9
North Peak 49, 50
North Peak Access Road 48-50
Ocean Shore Railroad 12, 13, 14, 15, 16, 18, 19, 37, 42, 44, 125, 130-143, 155, 157, 162
Oddstad, Andrew 36, 166
Old Pedro Mountain Road 45-47, 146, 150
Old Trout Farm Trail 28

Pacifica 120, 133
Peak Mountain 50
Pedro Point 13, 14, 18, 19, 157-159
Pedro Point headlands 15, 17
Plaskon Nature Trail 27
Portolá, Gaspar de 36, 117-118
Prohibition 15, 20, 146, 155
Railroads (paper) 143
Rancho Corral de Tierra Palomares 119-120
Rancho San Pedro 119-120
Red tides 22
Road Trail 121
Saddle Cut 16, 131, 133, 136, 156, 161
Saddle Pass 47, 115, 117 165, 166
San Pedro Creek 13, 27, 28, 33 49, 116
San Pedro Mountain (name) 9
San Pedro Terrace 13
San Pedro Valley 13, 36-37, 158-159
San Pedro Valley County Park 25, 37
Sanchez Adobe 37, 119
Sanchez, Francisco 37, 119
Sea Level Boulevard 146, 155-156
Shamrock Ranch 17, 44
Shelter Cove 13, 14, 15
Shipwrecks 19
South Peak 50
Spanish 36, 117-118
Steelhead Trout 13, 27
Sweeney Ridge 9, 36, 118
Tobin Depot 12, 13, 15, 131, 134
Valley View Trail 34
Weiler Ranch Road 33
World War II 21, 22, 43, 46, 51

Gum Tree Lane Books
Celebrates the San Mateo County Coast

Granada, A Synonym for Paradise:
The Ocean Shore Railroad Years by Barbara VanderWerf
[208 pages. 128 historical and recent photos. 3 aerial photos. 21 maps. 35 line illustrations. Bibliography. Index. ISBN: 0-9632922-0-X]

"I read *Granada, A Synonym for Paradise* with much interest and pleasure. ...a substantial job of researching a remarkably intriguing place, and [written] with grace and energy."
John R. Stilgoe, Harvard University

"The [Daniel H.] Burnham dream for El Granada versus what was built is like an award-winning movie script that never made it to the screen. ...a pillar of architecture left his mark on the small town of El Granada. ...a carefully documented [account]"
Bradley Inman, *San Francisco Examiner*

"*Granada, A Synonym for Paradise*...is worthy of notice. ...it is an invaluable source...the author writes extensively on the Ocean Shore Railroad..."
Harre W. Demoro, *San Francisco Chronicle*

"...a rich account...given immediacy and color by the liberal use of quotations from old newspapers, letters, essays and novels."
Matthew Brady, *San Francisco Independent*

"...more than just a regional history of California's small coast town of El Granada: it's an exploration of common railroad myths and realities which offers invaluable, detailed insights on early railroad growth. This volume tells what it was like to live on the San Mateo coast in the early 1900s, liberally peppering its story with vintage black and white photos. Fine, simple maps, chronologies, and community insights make for a handsome result: a probe of the Ocean Shore Railroad's history and its importance to the region. Few such titles offer the solid look, research, and appeal...it's highly recommended as a unique community and landscape history."
Diane Donovan, *Bookwatch, The Midwest Book Review*

"VanderWerf takes pride in her community and that pride shines brightly as she describes how El Granada came to be. ...[she] obviously took great pains to present an accurate account. It's worth a look."
    Rick Eymer, San Mateo *Times*

"People asking about the unusual reality of small villages dotting the San Mateo coastline can have their questions answered by VanderWerf's new book. ...chock-full of historical photographs and first-person anecdotes about the San Mateo County coast."
    Chris Hunter, *Pacifica Tribune*

"To VanderWerf, the history of El Granada and the railroad are inextricably linked. ...[her] fascination extends to what the railroad left behind—the old homes, the remnants of the railroad, the groves of blue gum eucalyptus and Monterey cypresses."
    Marc DesJardins, *Half Moon Bay Review*

"Delightful stories, poems and pictures on every page...for anyone interested in the history of the Coastside."
    Alice Jamieson, San Mateo County Historical Association

"The Ocean Shore line was so influential in developing the area that much of the book is devoted to it. ...I enjoyed the entire book."
    Bob Brown, *Narrow Gauge and Short Line Gazette*

"...fascinating account of a railroad built on the dreams of real estate barons and gone in a fraction of time. At $15.95 this is a bargain."
    Arthur L. Lloyd, *Western Railroader*

"...highly readable. ...well researched and crafted. ...highly recommended for anyone interested in either railroad history or 'landscape history' or both. READ IT!"
    Richard Mitchell, *Ferroequinologist*

The Coastside Trail Guidebook:
  Plants, Animals, Historical Lore along Half Moon Bay
  on the San Mateo County Coast by Barbara VanderWerf
[80 pages. Photos, maps and sketches. ISBN: 0-9632922-1-8]

"...does a marvelous job of presenting the Coastside—past, present and even a touch of tomorrow...gives depth to what a casual stroller would see walking the shore."
    Steve Tracy, *Half Moon Bay Review*

"Don't leave home without this remarkably all-inclusive book."
    Rick Eymer, San Mateo *Times*

Order Information

To order, please send check or money order to—

> Gum Tree Lane Books
> P.O. Box 1574
> El Granada, CA 94018

Montara Mountain	$12.95
CA sales tax (CA residents only)	1.06
Total	$14.01
The Coastside Trail Guidebook	$7.95
CA sales tax (CA residents only)	.66
Total	$8.61
Granada, A Synonym for Paradise	$15.95
CA sales tax (CA residents only)	1.32
Total	$17.27

Please add $2.00 shipping and handling for the first book ordered and $.50 for each additional title ordered.

Order form:

Title(s) _____ $_____.____

_____ $_____.____

_____ $_____.____

CA sales tax (CA residents only) _____ $_____.____

Shipping and handling _____ $_____.____

Total enclosed_____ $_____.____

Shipping address (please print)—

Name_____

Address_____

City_____

State_____ ZIP _____

Reflections

"I stood on Nature's balcony around the picturesque amphitheater formed by Montara Mountain with the sea and sky like a curtain fronting me. The sun was going down, the sky was alive with a riot of rose-red color. Some passing clouds were aflame, and flung their golden afterglow to the triple peaks that notch Montara's highest rim. The sun was large. It was near. The illusion was so great that if you stood at the shore you could reach your arms across the rippling green waves and burn your hands in its fire. The sky-edge trembled in response to the waves, and made the color rest uneven on the water. A real ship on the painted ocean sent skyward its spiral column of smoke, and rested anchorless between the sun and shore. The dark, ascending column was fringed with gold. The sun slipped into the water, a half-moon of sun only rose above the dark-green sea.

"I have seen the sun run an avenue of gold around the top of Popocatepetl; I have watched the gold on white as the sun complained with the peaks of Ranier; I have seen the icicles on the pines that crown the half-way summit of San Jacinto painted gold, like cathedral spires. I have seen the warm afterglow of the sun on the top of Shasta, that glittered like the porch of Heaven; I have watched the great red, red sun, a huge bird of fire, sink to rest in the desert sands—but God never touched with brush a finer painting than the large green-and-gold curtains that hung in front of the peaks of Montara that evening I saw the sun go down."

—M. B. Johnson. July 28, 1914. *San Mateo News*